Data science

The Ultimate Guide to Data Analytics, Data Mining, Data Warehousing, Data Visualization, Regression Analysis, Database Querying, Big Data for Business and Machine Learning for Beginners

Contents

PART 1: DATA SCIENCE 1

INTRODUCTION 1

CHAPTER 1: WHAT IS DATA SCIENCE? 2

CHAPTER 2: THE ART OF DATA SCIENCE 8

CHAPTER 3: DATA SCIENCE AS A CHANGE AGENT 13

CHAPTER 4: DATA SCIENCE TECHNIQUES 18

CHAPTER 5: DATA VISUALIZATION 24

CHAPTER 6: MACHINE LEARNING FOR DATA SCIENCE 28

CHAPTER 7: DATA SCIENCE AND BIG DATA ANALYTICS 33

CHAPTER 8: DATA SCIENCE TOOLS TOWARDS DATA SCIENCE 39

CHAPTER 9: DATA SECURITY – PROTECT MAJOR ENTERPRISE ASSETS 44

CHAPTER 10: MASTERING YOUR DATA WITH PROBABILITY 51

CHAPTER 11: DATA IN THE CLOUD 57

CHAPTER 12: ARTIFICIAL NEURAL NETWORKS 61

CHAPTER 13: DATA SCIENCE MODELING AND FEATURIZATION 64

CHAPTER 14: FIVE MINING TECHNIQUES DATA SCIENTISTS REQUIRE FOR THEIR OWN TOOLBOX 68

CHAPTER 15: THE CONCEPT OF DECISION TREES IN DATA SCIENCE 72

CONCLUSION 76

PART 2: DATA SCIENCE FOR BUSINESS 77

INTRODUCTION 78

CHAPTER 1: WHAT IS DATA SCIENCE? 79

CHAPTER 2: HOW BIG DATA WORKS IN DATA SCIENCE 85

CHAPTER 3: EXPLORATIVE DATA ANALYSIS 89

CHAPTER 4: WORKING WITH DATA MINING 91

CHAPTER 5: DATA MINING TEXT 94

CHAPTER 6: BASIC MACHINE LEARNING ALGORITHMS TO KNOW 98

CHAPTER 7: DATA MODELING 107

CHAPTER 8: DATA VISUALIZATION 110

CHAPTER 9: HOW TO USE DATA SCIENCE RIGHT 114

CHAPTER 10: TIPS FOR DATA SCIENCE 116

CONCLUSION 120

Part 1: Data Science

What the Best Data Scientists Know About Data Analytics, Data Mining, Statistics, Machine Learning, and Big Data – That You Don't

Introduction

Data is an important resource. However, if you do not have the right means to process it, then there is not much that you can benefit from regarding its value. Data Science is one of those multidisciplinary areas whose major focus is to derive value from data in all means. This book will explore the field of Data Science using data and its structure. In addition, it will describe high-level processes that one uses to change data into value.

You know that Data Science is a process. However, this does not mean that it lacks creativity. In fact, when you move deep into the stages of processing data, right from munging data sources to Machine Learning and finally data visualization, you will start to see that complex steps are involved in working with raw data.

The steps that one follows in transforming raw data into value also vary. For instance, in an explanatory analysis, you may have a cleaned data set that is ready to be imported into R, and you visualize the result but don't deploy the model.

Data comes in different forms, but at an advanced level, it exists in three major categories. Those categories are structured, semi-structured, and unstructured. Data Scientists are experts responsible for gathering, analyzing and interpreting large amounts of data to help businesses and organizations. Throughout all the chapters in this book, you are going to learn what the best Data Scientists know about Data Analytics, Machine learning, Big Data, Data Mining, and Statistics. Since Data Science is a multidisciplinary field, this book covers very critical concepts that you must know to become a Professional Data Scientist.

Chapter 1: What is Data Science?

The arrival of Big Data resulted in the expansion of storage space. As a result, storage became the biggest hurdle to most enterprises. Besides this, both organizations and enterprises are required to build a framework and develop a solution to store data. Therefore, Hadoop and other frameworks were developed to solve this problem. Once this issue was solved, the focus shifted to how data could be processed. When it comes to data processing, it is hard not to talk about Data Science. That is why it is important to understand what Data Science is and how it can add value to a business. This chapter will take you through the definition of Data Science and the role it plays in extracting important insights from complex data.

Why is Data Science Important?

Traditionally, data was structured in a small size. This means that there was no problem if you wanted to analyze data. Why? There were simple BI tools that you could use to analyze data. But modern data is unstructured and different from traditional data. Therefore, you need to have advanced methods of data analysis. The image below indicates that before the year 2020, more than 80% of the data will be unstructured.

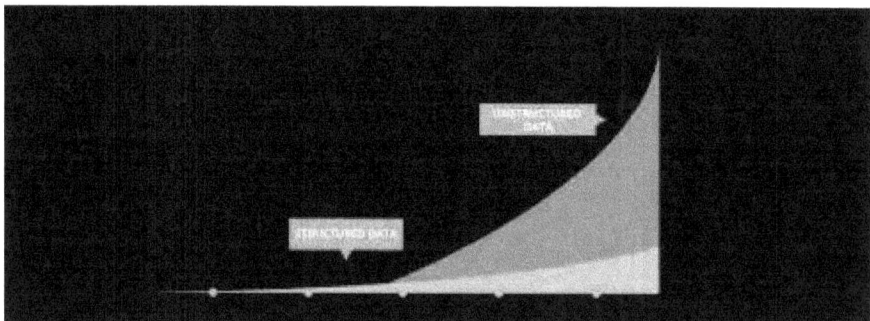

This data comes from different sources such as text files, financial logs, sensors, multimedia forms, and instruments. Simple BI tools cannot be used to process this kind of data as a result of the massive nature of data. For this reason, complex and advanced analytical tools and processing algorithms are required. These types of tools help a Data Scientist analyze and draw important insights from data.

There are still other reasons why Data Science has increasingly become popular. Let's take a look at how Data Science is applied in different domains.

Have you ever thought of having the ability to understand the exact requirements of your customers from existing data such as purchase history, past browsing history, income, and age? The truth is: now it is possible. There are different types of data which you can use to effectively train models and accurately recommend several products to customers.

Let's use a different example to demonstrate the role of Data Science in decision making. What if your car is intelligent enough to drive you home? That would be cool. Well, that is how the self-driving cars have been designed to work.

These cars gather live data from sensors to build a map of the surroundings. Based on this data, the car can make decisions such as when to slow down, when to overtake, and when to take a turn. These cars have complex Machine Learning algorithms that analyze the data collected to develop a meaningful result.

Data Science is further applied in predictive analytics. This includes places such as weather forecasting, radars, and satellites. Models have been created that will not only forecast weather but also predict natural calamities. This helps an individual to take the right measures beforehand and save many lives. The infographic presented below shows domains where Data Science is causing a big impact.

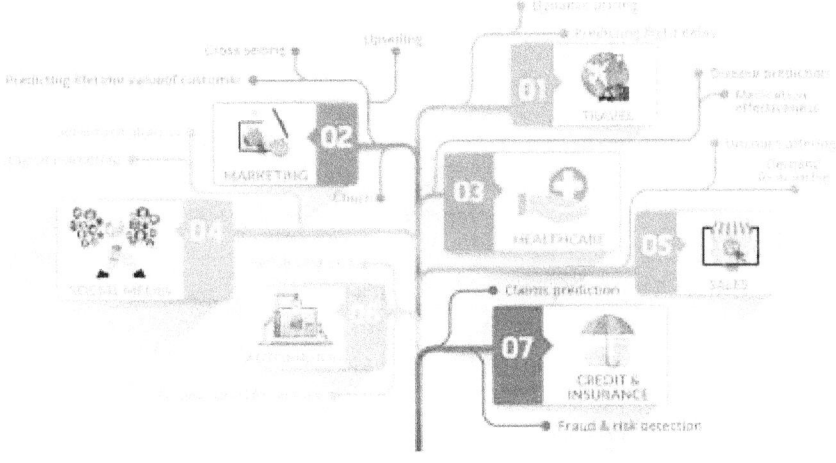

So, What is Data Science?

The term Data Science is common nowadays, but what does it mean? What skills does a person need to have to be called a Data Scientist? How are predictions and decisions made in Data Science? Is there a difference between Data Science and Business Intelligence? These are some of the questions that you are going to find answers to in a short while.

First, let's define Data Science.

Data Science refers to a combination of several tools, Machine Learning principles, and algorithms whose purpose is to discover hidden patterns from raw data. One might wonder how different it is from Statistics. The figure below has all the answers.

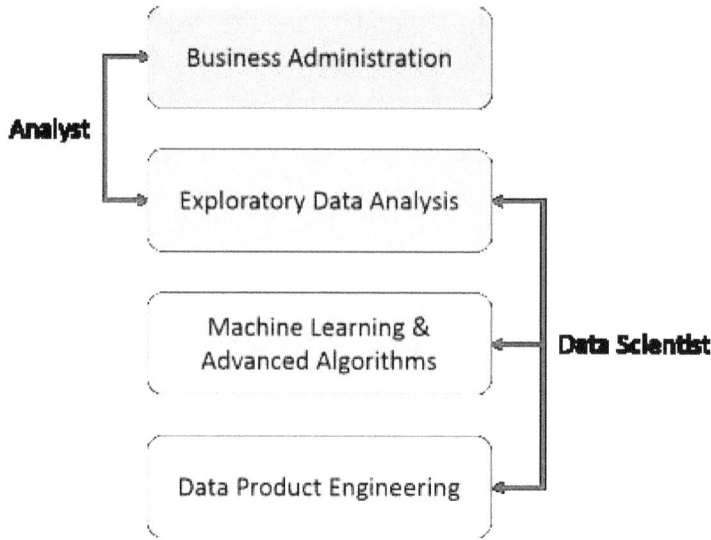

The figure above shows that a Data Analyst explains whatever is happening by processing history of the data. On the other hand, a Data Scientist will not only explain to extract insights from it, but they will also use different advanced Machine Learning algorithms to highlight the occurrence of a specific event in the future. A Data Scientist looks at the data from different perspectives and angles.

Therefore, Data Science helps an individual predict and make decisions by taking advantage of prescriptive analytics, machine learning, and predictive causal analytics.

• **Prescriptive Analytics.** If you need a model that has the intelligence and capability to make its own decisions, then prescriptive analytics is the best to use.

This new field delivers advice; it doesn't just predict, but it also recommends different prescribed actions and related outcomes. The best example to illustrate this is the Google self-driving car. Data that is collected by the vehicle is used to train the cars. You can further mine this data by using algorithms to reveal intelligence. This will allow your car to make decisions such as when to turn, which path to take, as well as when to speed up or slow down.

• **Machine Learning for Pattern Discovery.** Let's say that you don't have resources that you can apply to make predictions; it will require you to determine the hidden patterns in the data set to predict correctly. The most popular algorithm applied in pattern discovery is Clustering. Assume that you work in a telephone company, and you want to determine a network by installing towers in the region. Therefore, you may use the clustering technique to determine the tower location that will make sure all users have the maximum signal strength.

• **Make Predictions with Machine Learning.** If you want to build a model that can predict the future trend of a company, then Machine Learning algorithms are the best to go with. This falls under supervised learning; it is called supervised because data is already present that you can use to train machines.

• **Predictive Causal Analytics.** If you need a model that can help predict chances of a given event happening in future, you need to use the predictive causal analytics.

Data Science and Discovery of Data Insight

The main aspect of Data Science is to discover findings from data. It involves unearthing hidden insight that can allow companies to make smart business decisions. For example:

- Highlighting key customer segments inside its base as well as special shopping behaviors in the segments. This directs messages to different market audiences.

- Netflix extracts data from movie viewing patterns to find out what drives user interest and uses it to make decisions.

- Proctor and Gamble make use of time series models to understand future demand. This allows a person to plan for production levels.

But how do Data Scientists extract data insights? If you ever asked yourself this question, the answer is: it begins with data exploration. When faced with a difficult question, Data Scientists become curious. They attempt to find leads and understand characteristics within the data. To achieve this, an individual must have a higher level of creativity.

In addition, they may choose to use quantitative techniques to move deeper. Some examples are time series forecasting, inferential models segmentation analysis, synthetic control experiments, and many more. The aim is to put together a forensic view of what the data means. Hence, data-driven insight is the key in delivering strategic guidance. In other words, the role of Data Scientists is to guide business stakeholders so that they can learn how to respond to findings.

Development of a Data Product

A data product refers to a technical asset which makes use of data as input and processes the data to display the results of an algorithm. A classic example of a data product is a recommendation engine which takes user data and builds a personalized recommendation depending on the data. Below are examples of data products:

- A computer vision applied in self-driving cars

- Gmail's spam filter

- Amazon recommendation engine

This is not similar to "data insights" discussed previously where the final result is to generate advice to an executive team to help them make better business decisions. Conversely, a data product has a technical functionality that includes an algorithm and is developed to be encapsulated directly into the major applications. Some of the popular examples of applications that have a data product working behind the scenes are:

- Amazon's home page

- Gmail's inbox

- Autonomous driving software

Data Scientists play a major role in creating a product. This includes coming up with algorithms, testing, technical deployment, and refinement. In this case, Data Scientists act as technical developers who build assets which can be leveraged at a wide view.

Requisite Skillset for a Data Scientist

Mathematics Ability

At the center of mining data insight and developing a data product is the potential to see data through a quantitative lens. There are correlations, textures, and dimensions in data that one can represent mathematically. Developing solutions that make use of data involves heuristics and quantitative techniques.

Answers to most business problems include building analytic models that are grounded in the complex math where it is important to understand the principle behind the models.

Another misconception spread by people is that Data Science is mainly Statistics. Even though Statistics is critical in Data Science, it is not the only type of math learned. There are two categories of Statistics namely Bayesian Statistics and Classical Statistics. Most people tend to refer to Classical Statistics when they speak about stats. However, one is required to have knowledge of both types of Statistics. For instance, a common method to determine hidden characteristics in a data set is the SVD. This method is rooted in matrix math and has little to do with the classical stats. In general, it is good for Data Scientists to have both breadth and depth of mathematics knowledge.

Strong Business Acumen

It is good for a Data Scientist to have the traits of a tactical business consultant. By working alone with data, they have the edge to discover new concepts from data in ways that no one can. As a result, they have the task to translate observations that they see into a shared knowledge and recommend strategies in which they can solve major business problems. Therefore, a Data Scientist should be able to use data to create a story. The story has to be a cohesive narrative of the problem and solution.

Technology and Hacking

Hacking, in this case, refers to the creativity and ingenuity in the application of technical skills to define intelligent solutions to problems.

The ability to hack is important because Data Scientists make use of technology to amass massive data sets and work with advanced algorithms. This will need advanced tools rather than Excel. A Data Scientist has to develop quick solutions and integrate them with complicated data systems. The main languages linked with Data Science include SAS, Python, and R. Other languages include Julia and Java.

However, it is not just mastering the language that is the key. A hacker should be able to solve technical challenges creatively so that a program code can function correctly.

Furthermore, a Data Science hacker should have a solid understanding of the algorithm. They can break down difficult and messy problems so that they become solvable. This is very important because Data Scientists work in an environment of complex algorithms. Therefore, they should have a strong mindset to understand complex data.

Data Scientist – Curiosity and Training

The Mindset

A popular trait of most Data Scientists is that they think deep and have an intense intellectual curiosity. Data Science calls for one to be inquisitive. An individual has to regularly ask new questions, make new discoveries, and learn new things.

In fact, it is not money that drives them in their job but the ability to use their creativity to come up with solutions to problems and frequently engage in their curiosity. Extracting high dimensional leads from data goes just beyond making an observation. Instead, it is all about discovering the truth hidden beneath the surface. Data Scientists are grateful and passionate about what they do and find great satisfaction in taking on a challenge.

Training

There is a popular misconception that to be a certified Data Scientist, you must have a Ph.D. This view fails to consider that Data Science is multidisciplinary.

Chapter 2: The Art of Data Science

When it comes to data analysis, it is not as easy as it looks. One of the reasons why it is difficult is because only a few people have mastered the art of data analysis. This means that only a few people can explain how it is done.

Surprisingly, many people try to analyze data daily, but the majority fails in their efforts. This is because experts in this field haven't taken time to explain how they think while analyzing data.

Data Science is an art. It is not a concept that one can teach a computer. Data analysts use different tools to achieve their task, right from linear regression to classification trees. Even though all these tools are known to the computer, it is the role of the data analyst to figure out a way in which he or she can gather all the tools and integrate them to data to develop the correct answer to a question.

However, the process of data analysis has not been written down properly. While there are many books written about Statistics, none of them tries to address how one can create a real-world data analysis solution. On the other hand, coming up with an important framework involves classifying elements of data analysis using an abstract language. In some cases, this language might be mathematics. Conversely, the same details of the analysis are what make each analysis complex and interesting.

The Cycle of Analysis

You might look at data analysis and think that it follows a linear, step-by-step process that has a well-developed result. However, data analysis is an iterative and non-linear approach that is depicted by a series of epicycles. In this approach, information is learned at each step which then decides whether to redo and refine the next step that is already performed or proceed to the next step.

When it comes to analyzing data, the iterative process is used in all steps of the data analysis. Besides this, certain data analysis might appear fixed and linear because of the algorithms encapsulated in the different software.

Therefore, it is important that one understand what it means by the term "data analysis". Although a study of data involves creating and implementing a plan for gathering data, data analysis assumes that data is already gathered. Most importantly, a study will involve the creation of a hypothesis, designing of a data collection procedure, gathering of data, and interpretation of the data. However, since data analysis assumes that data should be collected already, it involves the development and refinement of a question and process of analyzing and interpreting data.

There are Five Major Activities of Data Analysis:

1. State and refine the question
2. Explore the data
3. Create formal statistical models
4. Interpret the results
5. Communicate the results

All the above activities happen on different occasions. For instance, it is possible to go through all of them in a day but handle each in detail in a period of more than one month. So, let's look at the overall framework applied in each of these activities.

While there are many different types of activities that one can engage in while performing data analysis, each aspect of the whole process can be undertaken through an interactive process. Most importantly, for each of the above five activities, it is advised that you include the following steps:

1. Define or set the expectations
2. Collect information and compare the data to your expectations
3. If the data fails to match your expectations, revise or fix the data so that both your expectations and data match

Going through all the three steps above is what is referred to as the cycle of the data analysis. While you navigate through every stage of the analysis, you will be required to go through the epicycle to constantly revise your question, formal models, interpretation, and communication. A repeated cycle through each of these five major activities forms the largest part of data analysis.

Define the Expectations

In this step, you intentionally lay down what you expect before you can do anything such as performing a procedure, inspecting your data or typing a command. For the experienced data analyst, creating expectations might be automatic or a subconscious process. Despite this, it is important to think about it. For instance, if you are going to shop with friends and you have to stop by an ATM to withdraw some money, you need to decide on the amount of money that you want to withdraw. You need to have some expectations of the price of the things you are going to buy. This could be something that you have no problem with if you know the price/s of the product/s you are going to buy. This is an example of prior knowledge. Another example of prior knowledge would be to know the time that a specific restaurant closes. Using that information, you can schedule your time and activities so that you show up for dinner before it closes.

You can also find out additional information from your friends that will help you come up with expectations or Google a restaurant to learn more about their working hours. This procedure that you apply on prior information to develop expectation or implement an analysis procedure is the same used in every main activity of the analysis process.

Information Collection

This step requires one to collect information related to the question or data. For questions, one collects information by doing a literature research or finding out from experts. For the data, once you have developed some expectations about what the result can be when the data is inspected, it is okay to go ahead and carry out the operation. The results of this activity include data that you need to collect and determine whether the collected data matches your expectations.

Comparison of Expectations

Once you have the data in your hands, the next step is to compare your expectations to the data. Here, there are two possible results:

1. Your cost estimations match the amount on the check

2. Your cost estimations fail to match

If both the cost estimations and amount match, then you can move on to the next activity. Alternatively, if your expectations cost 60 dollars, but the check is 30 dollars, then your expectations and data are different. In this case, there could be two possible reasons for the difference: the first is that you may have wrong expectations and you need to revise; and second, the check may be wrong and contains errors. One key indicator that can hint on the status of your data analysis is the easiness or difficultness to match the data you collected to your original expectations.

Volume, Velocity, and Variety

Big Data has various "V"s. The major ones include velocity, variety, and volume. Big Data surpasses the storage capacity of normal databases. The scale of data generated is massive. As of today, a huge amount of data is generated. One reason for this is because of the increase in interaction. Interaction is a new phenomenon besides just transaction of data. Data interaction comes from activities of the browser, personal digital recorders, and geo-location.

With the advent of the "internet of things", massive data is produced that humans spend their entire time trying to analyze.

A good Data Scientist should know how to control volume. He or she should know how to create algorithms that can intelligently use the size of the data effectively. Things acquire a new direction when you have gargantuan data because each similarity becomes important, and one can easily make false conclusions. In most business applications, extraction of correlation is enough. However, the right Data Science uses techniques that determine the cause based on these correlations.

Data velocity will always accelerate. There is an increase in Facebook posts, tweets, and financial information generated by many users at a higher speed. Velocity increases the volume of data and reduces the time of data retention. For example, a high-frequency trading activity depends on data streams and fast information. But the authenticity of the data reduces rapidly.

Lastly, data variety has gone deep. Models which depend on just a handful of variables can now produce hundreds of variables because of the increase in computing power. The rate of change in volume, velocity, and data variety is currently possible for new economic-metrics and various tools.

Machine Learning

Machine Learning refers to how systems learn from various types of data they process. It is possible to train a system based on particular data to make decisions. The training process occurs continuously to enable systems to make updates and enhance decision-making ability. Systems that use spam filters are a great example to demonstrate how Machine Learning is applied. These systems use a Bayesian filter to change decisions.

Therefore, it will continue to stay ahead of spammers. The ability to dynamically learn is important because it helps prevent spammers from gaming the filter. Credit approvals use neural-nets and are a great example of Machine Learning technique. Besides that, Machine Learning prefers data compared to judgments. Hence, a good Data Scientist should have a variety of both. Machine Learning has helped in finding answers to questions of interest, and it has further proved to be a game-changer. What makes Machine Learning very interesting is the four characteristics of machine intelligence:

1. It is built on a strong foundation of a theoretical breakthrough
2. It redefines the current economic paradigm
3. The final result is commoditization
4. It unearths new data from Data Science

Supervised and Unsupervised Learning

There are two broad ways that a system can learn: supervised and unsupervised learning.

Supervised learning is where a system makes decisions depending on the type of data entered. Automated credit card approvals and spam filters apply supervised learning to achieve their functions. The system is supplied with a historical data sample of outputs and inputs. Based on this type of data, the system establishes the relationship between the two using Machine Learning techniques. You will need to use your judgment to choose the best technique to handle the task.

Unsupervised learning happens when you only have input data (X) without a corresponding output variable. Unsupervised learning aims to build a model of the underlying structure in the data order so that you can learn more about the data. It is called unsupervised learning because there is no correct answer and teacher. Algorithms are left to decide and discover interesting structure in the data.

Cluster analysis is an example of unsupervised learning. Cluster analysis selects a group of entities each with a different attribute and divides the entity space based on how far or near the entities of the attributes are. This will rearrange and redefine data by labeling it using additional tags. Factor analysis is part of the unsupervised learning technique.

Predictions and Forecasts

Data Science involves making forecasts and predictions. However, there is a distinction between the two. Predictions focus on highlighting a single outcome. If a person says that "it will be cold tomorrow," he or she has predicted. But if they say that "the chance of tomorrow being cold is 40%," they shall have made a forecast. This is because a forecast provides outcomes in the form of probabilities.

Chapter 3: Data Science as a Change Agent

Data Science is a change agent. Even though it has not been realized yet, this should be the perfect time for organizations to be ready. Companies that plan to change in the next couple of years should position themselves by gathering the correct data and investing in analytics capacity.

The main thing to consider while building a predictive model is to establish whatever it is that you want to predict and gather massive data sets which will permit you to do so. Even though it is still far to realize the change in management by applying predictive models, organizations can remain on the right path by adopting the right tools and collecting accurate data.

Use Digital Engagement Tools

There are always new systems created to allow organizations to collect real-time feedback from employees. As of now, organizations can take advantage of these tools and help enhance their services. Most of these tools have been developed and installed with more functionality to reveal more information about an employee. These are tools which will indicate more than just what employees think every time. Most of these tools provide a relevant change to the management and can further let one determine whether a change is received equally across many locations.

By working with large travel tourism firms, it helps create a system for real-time employee feedback. This provides a chance to experiment with various change strategies in a particular population company. The real-time feedback implies that one has to learn quickly how communications and interaction tactics are received. Therefore, it optimizes the actions in days instead of weeks. This particular data is then fed into a predictive model that will help one to accurately identify actions that can improve the adoption of a new practice and behavior by a specific group of employees.

Commercial tools that are available include IQ polls and sampling groups of employees through a smartphone app on a weekly basis to extract real-time insights. Many of these tools generate a big change but the data stream produced is even more important. As a result, it is essential to deploy these tools to achieve the success that comes with a change in data-driven processes.

Social Media Analytics and Stakeholder Sentiment

Managers of change have another option to see past the limits of an enterprise to draw insights related to the impact of change programs. Customers, investors, and supplies are major stakeholders in the change programs. They have a likely chance to participate in social media and comment about the changes which a company plans to make.

Advances in linguistic text analysis imply that one can detect clues linked to actions and behavior from the choices of words that people use. Besides that, the use of certain phrases, articles, and pronouns can help an individual discover how the other party feels. By applying such tools to analyze emails of a company, it eases the process of finding out insights and reactions of employees to various changes implemented. Therefore, insights generated after analyzing the internal conversation in an organization will be stronger when it is combined with external social media data.

Recording a Reference Data Related to Change in the Current Projects

You will discover that most organizations focus on measuring fractional shifts in the inventory turns, operational performance, and manufacturing efficiency.

However, issues dealing with change have a low track performance. Even if projects have unique characteristics, there are many similarities when it comes to changing a system, improving a process and reorganizing projects. There is a chance to record information related to the team, how long it takes to implement and the tactics applied. Building a reference data set similar to this may not generate an instant gain, but the entire data set increases. Therefore, it becomes easy for one to build an accurate predictive model that can be helpful in changing an organization.

How Data is Important in Change

For many years, companies relied on data-driven techniques to select candidates fit for senior roles. Nowadays, retail businesses have also adopted predictive analytics to hire their employees.

As a result, these tools have improved the performance of a project and helped develop a new data set. Let's assume that every leader and member of a team was subjected to psychometric testing and evaluation before a project. The data produced from this testing can be useful in the identification of a causal model that can generate the correct change project.

Creation of a Dashboard

Each organization is imagined to have a bespoke dashboard, created together with the firm's leadership team. This reflects the priorities of the organization, future plans, and competitive position. By doing it this way, dashboards generate significant insights into a particular transformation investment created by the organization.

Most data that contributes to these signs are already available but not collected. There are clients of Change Logic that have developed a dashboard to identify attrition and recruitment in a must-win talent. This is not hard, but it helps to enlighten the managerial team on how to use data to make intuitive decisions. While it might take some time for such tools to be created, organizations need to begin to create dashboards. If possible, they should automate them. As of today, most of these dashboards are vulnerable to version control problems, internal politics, and human error. Computerizing the dashboards makes it objective and transparent.

While companies gather data and use Data Scientists to build accurate models, all managers of change must be confident to call Data Scientists to come and interpret procedures that allow firms to meet their goals.

Creation of metrics can't be easy because metrics aren't one-and-done installations. Instead, it is a commitment cycle to capture data, refine dashboards and create models. To develop a reliable data set takes time. Data quality is a critical problem that also calls for the presence of a shared data language that will make organizations realize that they are measuring the correct thing. This has been one of the major issues for Data Analytics in other fields.

Even if it might end up taking a lot of time, it will finally end the causal loop and produce a reliable prediction about how an action can alter a given metric. This will increase investment and change from a particular action to another data-informed perception. Change management helps shift a struggling project and recommends significant business results and how you can realize them.

Innovation Mindset

While organizations continue to shift to digital transformation methods, more teams that are knowledgeable about Data Science are being formed. So far, the major challenge for Chief Data Scientists involves positioning the Data Science function properly where a given organization need is to increase its current and future activities. This means that there is a need to recruit Data Science teams to completely interact with the business and adopt the operational backbone of the firm.

Data Science has no formal description. Its goal is to understand and analyze actual phenomena using data. This can highly vary from one industry to another. However, with experiences from both worlds, one can define Data Science as an integration of skills in programming, mathematics, and communication with the application of scientific method to a particular domain of knowledge. This practice can be summarized into different strategies:

Skillsets. This requires an individual to measure the readiness of analytics, talent management, spreading evidence-based culture, and application of Data Science processes.

Data sets. This often covers data governance, infrastructures, and strategic data sources.

Toolsets. This deals with the selection of the right Data Science tools and use of the best practices in the company or firm.

Mindset. This will collect all the animating principles that support the ethos of a Data Science function to create value and innovate at the center of a digital transformation.

Mindset is the main force that changes investments in Skillsets, Data sets, and Toolsets into a cultural and economic impact.

Below are a set of principles that act as a blueprint for how one can develop the mindset of innovation in Data Science.

1. Culture Before Technology

In the modern era of technological push, it is easy for anyone to be dragged into the technology trap. Some of these tools may result in distractions and short-term cosmetic results. Similar to other innovative teams, technology does not attract or retain talent in the Data Science. Instead, what drives people is the healthy culture which ensures everyone is satisfied, supported, and challenged in his or her jobs.

2. Stories and Not Sprints

In the early stages, projects should have a buy-in from the leadership so that they can deal with anti-change agents and handle unrealistic expectations. With the advent of Agile methodologies, most firms have turned to sprints. However, innovation calls for both time and patience. Stories are an amazing way that one can create the right focus over time and build patience for teams to help in the execution. Demos, visualizations, and other types of stories motivate Data Science teams to wait, ask questions, and concentrate on visions than planning for a sprint. Narratives deliver the right chance to think deeply and consider a given business via interactions, system dynamics as well as how the change in analytical capability might affect an organization. The material generated furthermore act as a link to share knowledge outside the organization and across disciplines. It champions for a positive and creative spirit.

3. Ethics and Not Profits

Since the practice of Data Science is popular, teams should develop a moral direction and techniques that predict the limits of their discoveries. In addition, it is part of their leadership duty to assist in determining a social mission of the developed algorithm and analytics. It calls for collaboration to ensure the use of Data Science.

For instance, at the Massachusetts Institute of Technology (MIT), urban demos provided a means where one has to explore whether the concepts are culturally or socially acceptable before they were potentially profitable. By championing for initiatives that would result in social good and at the same time align people before profit, it helps enrich the analytical capacities with members that may not have participated in the commercial ventures.

4. Polymathy Before Expertise

Data Science includes a multidisciplinary concept and cannot work in isolation. To ensure that you can collaborate with other parties, specialists must learn beyond their domain expertise. There are certain organizations which may fall into the trap that it is a must to have a Ph.D. to do Data Science. This is not true because this practice calls for one to have an enhanced sense of curiosity to help learn the language of other disciplines and an in-depth appetite for collaborative learning. These are some of the traits of a polymath that makes a team ready to interact with people with diverse roles in the organization from design, product management, communication, finance, and many more. Of late, terms such as AI Designer and Product Scientist have risen in the industry to emphasize the importance of connecting different disciplines with the scientific method. At the same time, specific views from interdisciplinary domains such as science, technology, data bias and algorithmic have become part of the major themes of Data Science.

A generalized specialist will deliver an interdisciplinary knowledge that champions for creativity and a deeper understanding of what an organization or society needs. A team made up of generalized specialists present a better general perspective for complex, deep, and unconventional areas compared to a team of experts.

Chapter 4: Data Science Techniques

No matter what your opinion is about the subject of Data Science, it is very hard to look down upon the role of data and the ability to analyze, gather and contextualize data.

Not only that but with the development of Machine Learning technology and the emergence of fields such as Deep Learning that prove to be of importance to researchers, Data Scientists continue to enjoy innovations and technological developments.

Although a strong coding skill is critical, Data Science includes software engineering concepts. Data Scientists should have a mixture of coding, critical thinking, and statistical ability. He or she should be a good statistician as well as good at programming.

It is advised that one understands the ideas behind different techniques so that they know how and when to use them. It is critical for a person to understand simple methods so that they can understand complex ones.

Additionally, it is good to check the efficiency of a given method to discover whether it is working well or bad. This is an interesting field of research that has significant applications in science, finance, and industry. In general, Statistics is a major component that any successful Data Scientist must know.

Examples of Statistical Learning problems include:

- Personalize an email spam detection system.

- Find out whether an individual has a heart attack depending on the clinical measurements, demographic data, diet, and clinical measurement.

- Classify a sample of tissue into different cancer classes.

- Identify the relationship between demographic variables and salary in the population survey.

Before you start to read the techniques that any Data Scientist should learn so that they can be effective at dealing with large data sets, it is important to know the difference between statistical learning and machine learning. In the coming chapters, you will understand more about Machine learning. For now, here are some of the differences:

- Statistical learning started as a branch of Statistics.
- Machine Learning started as a branch of AI.
- Statistical learning concerns models and their interpretability, uncertainty, and precision.
- Machine Learning has an added advantage in Marketing.

1. Linear Regression

In terms of Statistics, linear regression predicts a target. This is achieved by fitting the right linear relationship between the independent and dependent variables. The perfect fit occurs when the sum of all distances between the shape and previous observations is small. The shape of the fit is the best because there is no other position which can produce the minimum error. Linear regression is divided into two types.

- Simple Linear Regression
- Multiple Linear Regression

In simple linear regression, there is a single independent variable which predicts a dependent variable by fitting the finest linear relationship. On the other hand, multiple linear regression contains more than one independent variable to predict a dependent variable.

2. Classification

This is a Data Mining technique that assigns features to a set of data to allow accurate analysis and predictions. Classification is very popular in the analysis of an advanced data set. The most common classification techniques include:

- Logistic Regression
- Discriminant Analysis

Logistic Regression

This type of analysis is best to use when you have a binary dependent variable. It is used to describe data and explain the association between one independent binary variable and a nominal independent variable.

Discriminant Analysis

Here, clusters have been known as a priori. Besides that, new observations are classified into a particular population based on the types of features measured. This method models the distribution of X predictors independently in every response class. Bayes' theorem is then used to estimate the probability of a response class. These models can either be linear or quadratic.

Quadratic Discriminant Analysis. This analysis contains an alternative choice. Similar to QDA, this analysis assumes that observations drawn from a class of Y come from the Gaussian distribution. Another assumption is that each class has a covariance matrix.

Linear Discriminant Analysis. This technique determines "discriminant scores" for each observation detected by linear combinations of independent variables. Here, it is also assumed that all observations recorded in each class come from a multivariate Gaussian distribution.

3. Subset Selection

This method will search for a subset of p predictors similar to the response. Next, a model is created by taking the least number of squares of the subset features.

The Best Subset Selection. Here, a different regression OLS is applied for each possible combination of p predictors and an observation of the model fit. The algorithm has two stages:

- Fit a model with k predictors.
- Highlight a model using a cross-validated prediction.

One should not forget to use validation error because RSS and R^2 increase monotonically as variables increase. The best way to use is to cross-validate and model using the highest R^2 and lowest RSS on determining the error estimates.

Forward Stepwise Selection. This technique considers a smaller subset of p predictors. It begins with a model without predictors and adds predictors to the model until that point when all predictors exist in the model.

Backward Stepwise Selection. This begins to work with predictors in the model and then removes the lowest predictor each time.

4. Shrinkage

This is the best to use for models which all have predictors. However, estimate coefficients are reduced to zero depending on the least squares estimates. Shrinkage also reduces the variance. Depending on the type of method used, some coefficients can be approximated to zero. The most popular shrinking techniques are lasso and ridge regression.

Ridge Regression. This is similar to the least squares with the only difference being the estimate of the coefficients. Ridge regressions select coefficient estimates that reduce RSS. But it has a penalty when the coefficients approach zero. This penalty can reduce the estimate of the coefficient to zero. That is why it is important to know that ridge regression removes traits with the smallest column space variance. The problem with ridge regression is that it has all p predictors available in the final model. In addition, the penalty term sets the rest of the predictors to zero. Usually, this is not a problem when you want to predict accurately, but it can make the model difficult to interpret the results. Lasso has the answer to this problem because it can force specific coefficients to move to zero as long as it is small.

5. Dimension Reduction

This reduces the issue of approximating p + 1 coefficient to a simple problem of M + 1 coefficient. In this case, M< p. You can achieve this by computing M different linear combinations and variable projections. In this case, M projections are extracted and used as predictors for a linear regression model. The most popular approaches that one can apply include partial least squares and component regression.

Principal Components Regression

This technique helps an individual extract a low-dimensional set of properties from a large group of variables. The first principal component (PC) direction of data has observations that change a lot. This means that the first PC represents a line that fits close to the data. It is possible for one to fit p distinct principal components. The next PC refers to a linear combination of variables that are different from the first PC and contain the largest variance subject of the constraint. The point is that the principal components retain the most variance in the data by applying a linear combination of the data in subsequent orthogonal directions. Therefore, it is correct to combine the effects of associated variables to find more information from the available data.

This method involves highlighting linear combinations of X which represent the best X predictors. This means that the combinations are unsupervised because the response Y is important in determining the principal component directions.

In other words, Y response cannot supervise the selection of the principal components. Hence, it is not a guarantee that the directions which define the predictors can be used to predict a response.

A Partial Least Square is an alternative to supervised. It is a mechanism which selects a new smaller set of features that contain a linear combination of previous features. Unlike PCR, Partial Least square uses the response variable to highlight the new features.

6. Nonlinear Models

In a nonlinear regression analysis, observational data is modeled using a nonlinear combination function of the model parameters. Additionally, it relies on more than one independent variable. In this method, data is applied by using successive approximations. Below are a few techniques that you can use to handle nonlinear models:

- **A Piecewise Function.** This function is defined with the help of multiple sub-functions which apply a specific interval of the main function's domain. Piecewise is a way in which one can express the function instead of the characteristic function itself.

- **A Spline.** This refers to a special function defining piecewise using a polynomial. In computer graphics, spline represents a piecewise polynomial parametric curve. Spline refers to popular curves as a result of simplicity in the construction.

7. The Tree-Based Methods

You can use this method in regression and issues related to classification. Some of these issues include segmenting the predictor space to build simple regions. Since a set of splitting rules is used in the predictor space, you can decide to summarize that into a tree. This type of approach is called a decision-tree method. Below are some of the most common tree methods:

- **Bagging.** This refers to the way one can reduce the variance of the prediction by producing extra training data from the initial data set. This is realized through a mix of repetitions that produce a multistep of similar carnality. If you can manage to increase the size of the training set, then you will have decreased the variance.

- **Boosting.** This method computes the output using different models and averages the result through a weighted average technique. By integrating the merits and pitfalls of the following technique, you can develop a good predictive force to be applied in a large size of input data.

- **Random Forest**. This algorithm resembles bagging algorithm. In this algorithm, an individual can develop random bootstrap samples of the training set. Besides the bootstrap samples, you can also build a random subset of features to use to train individual trees. In bagging, each tree is assigned a full set of features because of the random feature selection. In addition, an individual can make the trees more independent of each other rather than the regular bagging that usually leads to better predictive performance.

8. Support Vector Machines (SVM)

The Support Vector Machine is a classification technique categorized below the supervised learning models in the Machine Learning. In a different language, it is used to calculate the hyperplane in higher dimensions such as 2D and 3D. A hyperplane is defined as an n-1 dimensional subspace of an n-dimensional space which best differentiates two classes of points that have the maximum margin. Basically, it is a constrained optimization problem in which the margin is optimized.

The data points which support the hyperplane lie on either side and are called support vectors. In situations where there is inseparable data, the points have to be defined to a higher dimensional space where linear separation might be possible. A problem that consists of multiple classes can be divided into various one-versus-one binary classification problems.

9. The Unsupervised Learning

In unsupervised learning, groups of data are not known. This is left for the learning algorithm to determine the patterns in the provided data. Clustering is a great example of unsupervised learning where different data sets are grouped into groups that are closely related.

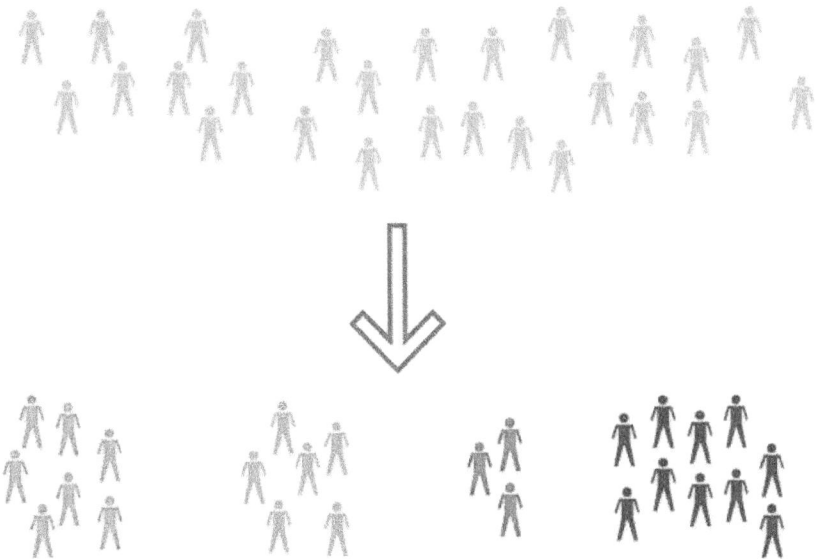

Principal Component Analysis. This is method will help you generate the least dimensional representation of the data set. The data set is produced by defining a set of linear properties that have a maximum variance and are mutually unrelated. This linear dimensionality approach could be important to help a person understand latent interaction in the unsupervised setting.

Hierarchical Clustering. This develops a multilevel hierarchy of clusters by building a cluster tree.

K-means Clustering. This will partition data into K distinct cluster depending on the distance to the centroid of a cluster.

This is a skeleton of basic statistical techniques that can assist a Data Science program manager to develop a better understanding of what is happening besides Data Science terms. The truth is that there are certain Data Science terms which run algorithms via R and python libraries. Despite this, if you can understand the basics of statistical analysis, it will provide your team with a better approach. Develop insight related to the smallest parts to support easy abstraction and manipulation.

Chapter 5: Data Visualization

When you want to understand, and discover important data insights, a picture turns out to be an essential tool. Visuals are helpful when you want to discover relationships between hundreds of variables.

Companies produce and gather data every minute. Everyone from data analysts to employees wants to pick up something from the different sets of data which can help a person make a better decision and work more effectively.

No matter the size of the data you have, the best way to master important relationships is through complex analysis and an easy to understand visualization. No one wants to miss any critical correlation or develop the wrong conclusion that might heavily affect their decision making. When complex analysis is rapidly carried out, the outcome can be displayed in a way that is simple to use as well as allow exploration and queries. As a result, everybody in the organization has the chance to dig deep into data and develop insights for faster and effective decisions.

To develop some significant visuals from data, there are standard things one needs to consider. Some of these things include data type, data size, and column composition.

Data Scientists work with a large data set. One of the greatest challenges that they face is determining which method to use to show data. You may need to condense and collapse data. However, you will still need to display graphs and charts that most decision makers know. Don't forget that in the current society, visualization is essential. Therefore, ensure that it is well-displayed in smartphones.

At the same time, it is good to give people the freedom to interact with data in real time. For instance, SAS Visual Analytics supports several business customers to draw significant insights from data without having any Data Science skill.

Intelligent and auto-charting tools facilitate the creation of the best visual based on the type of data highlighted. These tools will identify the relevant findings without asking users to write algorithms. Additionally, smart visualization will allow Data Scientists and analysts to build prototypes quickly and reduce the time spent on experiments.

Charting

Line Charts

Line charts reveal the existing relationship between variables. These charts also track the relationship between one variable and another one. If you have a lot of items and want to make some comparisons, then a line chart is the best approach to use. Why? It has stack lines that best draw comparisons of individual values for different variables.

An individual may choose to apply a line chart when there is a variable change, or a variable has to be displayed, and rate-of-change of information is of value. It is important also to note that because in a line chart you have the data points, there is no need to choose a line chart. However, depending on the number of data points that you have, it will determine the type of visual to use. So, if you want to know whether to use a line chart or not, count the number of data points that need to be displayed.

Bar Charts

Bar charts are the best when you want to make comparisons between quantities of different groups. Values belonging to a particular category are shown using bars and then displayed as a vertical bar or horizontal bar.

In case the values are distinct, it is easy to notice the difference in the bars by how they look to our eyes. However, if the values are very close or there are a large number of values to be displayed, it becomes hard to compare bars.

To ensure that there is some visual difference, you can assign the bars different colors. The colors can reveal things such as status or range. If you decide to color the bars, it will look beautiful and smart. The different colors will allow viewers to see the differences between bars.

There are different kinds of bar charts. For instance, the progressive bar chart shows how a measure of an original value can increase or decrease during a transaction. The first bar starts at the initial value, and each subsequent bar resumes from where the initial bar ends. This bar has a length and direction to indicate the magnitude and type of transaction.

Scatter Plots

A scatter plot is a two-dimensional plot which describes a shared difference of two data items. Each marker in a scatter plot is an observation. The position of the marker will reveal the value of each observation.

You should use scatter plots when you want to create a relationship between X and Y variables. The variables are said to be correlated when there is a dependency, and every variable can affect another one. For example, there is a relationship between profit and revenue.

The relationship could be that any time revenue increases, profit also increases. A scatter plot is the best tool to use to visualize relationships in data. Scatter plot allows a person to use statistical analysis by combining correlation and regression. Correlation is important to help an individual identify the extent of a statistical correlation between every variable in the plot. On the other hand, regression allows a person to define the relationship between variables in the plots.

Once all data points have been plotted, you can move on to identify data points that have a specific relationship. Using a scatter plot, it will help you develop an idea of how you can spread out the data present in the distributions. It is recommended to use scatter plots when you have a lot of data points. However, if you have a small data set, a table could be effective to help display the information.

Bubble Plots

These are a type of scatter plot where markers are identified with bubbles. A bubble plot will reveal the relationship between three measurements. If you have two measurements, you can use plot axes to highlight. The third measure is defined with the help of a bubble.

It is better to use a bubble plot when you have hundreds of data values. You can choose to apply color to illustrate extra measurements and animate the bubbles to demonstrate changes in the data. A geo bubble map is displayed on a geographic map. Each bubble is set up at a specific geographic location.

Pie and Donut Charts

There has been a huge discussion around pie and donut charts. Both help an individual to create comparisons between parts. But it is difficult to notice because the eyes of a human being cannot easily estimate areas and compare visual angles. So, if you decide to use a chart, you will find it hard to compare data that is similar in size.

If you build a dashboard, you are advised to consider how a donut chart or pie chart works. The efficiency of a pie or donut chart is revealed by the amount of space that a chart needs to size a report. Since these charts are round, most of them will require additional space.

In general, there are many types of charts that one can pick to show and analyze data. The choice to use a chart depends on the number of measures that an individual would like to visualize.

How to Visualize Big Data

Big Data presents specific problems when you want to visualize data because of the speed, size, and diversity of the data.

The most common definition of Big Data consists of three important terms: velocity, volume, and variety. SAS Visual Analytics has a creative approach to handle issues to do with Big Data visualization. The use of in-memory capabilities integrates SAS Analytics to reveal new ways of representing and analyzing data.

Dealing with Large Data Volumes

Let's face it: Data Scientists find it hard when they want to present the results of a data exploration and analysis. One could be forced to apply a new method of reviewing data and intuitively combine results. You might also be required to display the available results through a mobile device and support users who want to explore data in real time.

To work with a vast size of data is not that easy; you may find it hard to understand, and as a result, it is advised to use better visualization tools. The auto-charting function built in SAS Visual Analytics reviews data based on the size and type of data. It is the best visualization tool to use. For that reason, business analytics and employees can easily use this tool to visualize data. It will help them create a hierarchy of data and explore data in a very interactive manner.

The volume of data can be a problem because traditional architecture and software may not define a vast size of data promptly.

Still, the most popular descriptive Statistics calculations can be complicated when handling Big Data. For instance, if a data set has a billion rows and you want to build a scatter plot that contains two measurements, it can be hard to see numerous data points. Similarly, the type of application that helps an individual visualize the data may fail to work. The only other solution that one can resort to is binning. Binning requires an individual to gather data from both axes so that they can visualize the Big Data in the most effective manner.

A box plot describes a geographical display of five Statistics. The five Statistics consists of medial, lower quartile, upper quartile, maximum and minimum. All the above five Statistics are important when you want to create a summary to define the distribution of a set of data.

Usually, box plots prove effective to Data Scientists because it identifies abnormal points called outliers. Generally, the percentage of outliers in data ranges between 1-5%. For the traditional size data sets, this particular data proportion is not hard to notice. However, for those working with a vast data set, it can be very hard to identify.

How to Visualize Semi-structured and Unstructured Data

The difference in Big Data leads to several challenges. These challenges exist because both structured and semi-structured data requires visualization techniques. A word cloud visual can be applied to unstructured data to help indicate the frequency of words. This can either be low or high.

In the SAS Visual Analytics, word clouds are important in the classification and creation of associations. The words are further classified into topics depending on the way the words are used.

Data Scientists also use network diagram to visualize semi-structured data. The network diagrams examine relationships based on nodes that represent relationships between individuals. The networks in network diagram have nodes which represent points while ties represent lines.

You can use network diagrams in different disciplines and applications. For example, businesses that analyze social networks discover interactions with customers.

Chapter 6: Machine Learning for Data Science

Machine Learning refers to an analytic data method that trains computers to perform something that comes naturally to both humans and animals. It is all about learning from experience. Machine Learning algorithms have computational methods to help an individual discover information from data without waiting for a predetermined equation. These algorithms dynamically improve the performance of data when the number of samples available for learning increases.

Why is Machine Learning important?

An increase in Big Data makes Machine Learning an essential method to solve problems such as:

- Image processing and computer vision
- Energy production for load forecasting
- Computational finance for algorithmic trading and credit scoring
- Natural language processing to help recognize a voice
- Aerospace, automotive, and manufacturing for predictive maintenance

Machine Learning algorithms identify natural patterns in data to draw insight and make smart decisions. It is used daily to make critical decisions in stock trading, medical diagnosis, and forecasting.

Examples of Machine Learning application include media sites that analyze customer data before suggesting possible movies that a user can download or view. Additionally, retailers have to draw significant information in the manner in which customers buy products.

When is it Right to Apply Machine Learning?

When you are about to work on a complex task or issue, that is the perfect time to apply Machine Learning.

The Real Deal about Machine Learning

Machine learning has its limits. It is not possible to build intelligent machines such as in *Star Trek* and *2001: A Space Odyssey*'s Hal 9000. But there are many examples of real-world processing applications where Machine Learning operates like a charm. Below are popular categories where Machine Learning is applied:

Image Processing

It requires one to analyze images and get data or perform certain transformations. Examples include:

- **Image Tagging.** This is similar to Facebook where an algorithm can automatically identify your face or the face of your friends in a photo. Basically, a Machine Learning algorithm will learn from the photos that are manually tagged.

- **Optical Character Recognition.** Once an algorithm learns how to change a scanned text document into a digital version, the algorithm must know how to change an image into a written character of the corresponding digital letter.

Text Analysis

This is the process in which information is classified or extracted from emails, documents, chats, and tweets. Popular examples include:

- **Sentiment Analysis.** It is another application area of text classification. In this type of classification, an algorithm must know how to classify an opinion as neutral, positive or negative depending on the mood displayed by the writer.

- **Information Extraction.** It involves learning to extract a given piece of information or data.

- **Spam filtering.** It is one of the most widely used text classification application. Spam filters help classify an email as spam based on the content and subject.

Data Mining

This is a method used to determine predictions from data. The definition appears generic, but one can look at it as extracting important information from a massive table in a database. Every row would consist of training instances and a column feature. You could be interested in forecasting a new column in the table that relies on the rest of the columns. For instance:

- **Association Rules**. Take the example of a supermarket or an e-commerce site. It is possible to determine customer purchasing habits by taking a look at the type of products bought together. This type of information can be useful for marketing purposes.

- **Anomaly Detection.** Look for outliers. For instance, in the credit card fraud detection, you may identify the type of transactions and outliers from the normal purchasing pattern of a user.

- **Predictions.** This involves prediction of a variable from the rest of the variables. For instance, you can predict the credit score of new customers in the bank by learning from the credit score and profiles of current customers.

Steps in the Application of Machine Learning

Every Machine Learning task is divided into several steps:

1. Choose the Machine Learning Approach

Before you can begin any steps, a Machine Learning problem must be expressed. Ask yourself what you want to find out? Do you want to categorize data, predict new values or group data based on some factors? Once you choose the type of Machine Learning task you want to perform, you can move on and select the model.

2. Collect Data

In this step, you can choose to write data on paper, store spreadsheets in an SQL database, and record text files. The data collected should be in an electronic format to make it easy to analyze.

3. Explore and Prepare Data

The effectiveness of a Machine Learning project is defined by the quality of data that it uses. It is recommended that 80% of the effort generated in ML be directed to data preparation. This step calls for a great deal of human intervention.

4. The Training Model on the Data

The right Machine Learning task will identify the right algorithm. You can then feed the data into the model during this stage. A learner refers to a Machine Learning algorithm trained on some data and adjusted to suit the data in the best possible means.

5. Evaluate the Performance of a Model

Since each learner generates a biased solution, it is good to determine the best way in which an algorithm learns from its experience. Based on the model applied, you could be able to determine the accuracy of the learner by using a test data set.

6. Enhance Model Performance

In case a better performance is required, it is good to use an advanced mechanism to improve the performance of a model.

Once these steps are over and the model seems to work well, it is deployed for its required task. The model can be used to generate scores for predictions, projected values for novel data, and important insight for research and marketing.

It is essential to track the success and failures of a deployed model to help an individual produce additional data to train the next generation model.

Select a Machine Learning Algorithm

The type of Machine Learning algorithm you choose depends on the data present and the proposed task at hand. It is critical to think about this process during the collection of data, exploration, and data cleaning.

Input Data

All Machine Learning algorithms need to have some training data. Training data is available in the form of features and examples.

An **example** includes a single exemplary instance of the underlying concept learned. It refers to a single set of data that describes the atomic unit of interest applied in the analysis. In case you are developing a learning algorithm to select spam email, the examples would include data from electronic messages. For one to identify cancer tumors, examples may need to comprise biopsies from different patients.

A **feature** refers to a characteristic or example of an attribute. It can be important for learning the correct concept. In the previous example, attributes in the spam detection data set might include words applied in the email messages and domain names. In the cancer data set example, it could be genomic data from biopsied cells or even a measured characteristic of the patient such as age, weight, blood pressure, and height.

Features are available in different forms. If a feature reveals a characteristic measured in numbers, it is referred to as numeric. For instance, weight and height are numeric. At the same time, if there is a feature which determines an attribute represented by a set of classifiers, the feature is referred to as nominal or categorical. If the following categories have a specific order, then the feature is referred to as ordinal. It is vital to pay attention to what these features represent because both the number and type of features in the data set assist in defining the correct Machine Learning algorithm.

Machine Learning Algorithms

They are two types: supervised learners and unsupervised learners. You already know one or two things about these two types of algorithm. In brief, supervised learners create a predictive model while unsupervised learners build a descriptive model. Which type a Data Scientist should select depends on the task at hand and what he or she needs to achieve.

A predictive model is the best to use if you have tasks that alter the prediction of one value by applying another value in the data set.

The learning algorithm will try to identify and model the association between the target feature and other features. Predictive models don't require one to forecast future events.

Since predictive models have a detailed instruction of what is required to learn based on positive and negative instances, this process is described as supervised learning. In this case, supervision does not describe human involvement, but the target values deliver a supervisory role that guides the learner in whatever they need to learn. Most importantly, when given a set of data, the algorithm will try to optimize a function to determine a combination of feature values that generate the target output.

The target feature that should be predicted is a categorical feature referred to as a class and is made up of different categories called levels. A class can consist of multiple levels.

Supervised learners can further help predict numeric values such as laboratory values, income, and test scores. To predict these numeric values, linear regression models are applied. Even though regression models are not the only model, they are the most commonly used models.

A descriptive model is used to handle tasks that could generate insight gained from data summarization. Although it predicts a specific target of interest, it is different because no single feature is more important than another.

Given that a descriptive model does not have a target to learn, the procedure of training a descriptive model is called unsupervised learning. These methods are good for one to use to mine data. Example of descriptive modeling is pattern discovery. This method allows one to identify common relations in data. Pattern discovery is very common in market basket analysis. The most important task carried out in market basket analysis is to select products which customers like to purchase in pairs.

In the modern world, data sets continue to expand and increase in complexity. Machine Learning methods have become important in the biomedical community and building predictive models. Most researchers aren't well trained to build and interpret these models. Therefore, it can be very difficult to select the right approach to a given data set.

It is essential to identify the goal of a study so that you can determine whether it needs supervised or unsupervised learning. For instance, if the main goal is to develop a model that can predict the disease status of a patient, it is right to use a supervised approach. Choosing to use an unsupervised method, such as clustering, can mix the signal and produce the worst predictor. Conversely, if the goal is to develop an overview of a data set to determine the strongest patterns and whether the samples can be divided into subgroups, then the unsupervised method should be applied.

Another factor to remember when adopting supervised methods is that you will have to search explicitly for patterns related to the annotation you want to predict. It is likely that you will discover something in the vast data space which can predict the annotation in the current data set. But this is not what you are aiming at. However, you are interested in determining whether a specific model can generalize. Therefore, supervised models should always be validated in independent data sets. Additionally, a good predictive performance in the training data does not mean that a model is good.

Chapter 7: Data Science and Big Data Analytics

Regardless of whether you are going to enhance the supply chains, monitor floor operations, measure consumer sentiment or any large scale analytic problems, Big Data has a huge effect on the enterprise. The size of business data produced has increased by a huge value each year, and various types of information are stored in digital formats.

One of the biggest challenges involves learning how you can handle new data types and discover the type of information that offers value to your business. It is not just about how you can access new data sources, but the inter-relationships among elements and patterns are also important. Gathering different types of data rapidly does not produce value. You must use analytics to discover insights which will support the business.

Big Data does not create new storage mechanisms and new data types, but it develops new analyses. This chapter will define Big Data analysis and review different ways that one can analyze Big Data to develop patterns and relationships. In addition, you will learn how to make informed predictions and derive business insight from a huge influx of information.

It is important to note that Big Data is not an independent set of activities. Therefore, you require a cohesive set of solutions to help in Big Data analysis, collect data, and discover new insights to help make frequent decisions. Most organizations achieve their tasks by application of both commercial and open source components. Building an integrated architecture for Big Data analysis enables a person to perform different types of activities and transfer data among components.

Big Data? How does it matter?

Big Data describes data sets that have a size that surpass the normal function of database software tools such as storage, capturing, and analyzing.

It refers to a collection of data sets that are very large and complex such that one cannot process using simple database management tools.

Big Data Analytics

The term Big Data Analytics has widely been used in the market today. In most cases, it is used together with other related concepts such as Data Mining and Business Intelligence. While all these terms refer to how data is analyzed, Big Data is not the same when several transactions, data volumes, and data sources become big and complex. In this situation, specific methods and technologies are required to extract insight from data.

This leads to the general definition of Big Data which includes the three V: Velocity, Variety, and Volume.

- *Volume.* Refers to a large data set.

- *Variety.* Describes data that comes from different data sources. It is possible to have data that originates from external and internal data sources. The most important thing is that the data can be in any format. It can be log data or even structured data from database tables and semi-structured data such as XML.

- *Velocity.* Describes large sizes of data from transactions featuring higher refresh rates in data streams that have a higher speed and time.

From the above description, Big Data can be considered as a high-velocity, high-volume, and high variety information repository that require a cost-effective and innovative means of information processing. This process leads to improved insight, better decision making, and improved process automation.

Up to this point, it should be obvious that Big Data is not just about how large the data is volume, but the data should also arrive at a fast speed and in a complicated form. In addition, it should arrive from different sources.

Most important, it is good to highlight that there could be much value in attempting to define the elements that constitute Big Data. Every individual should know that the Big Data of today may not be the same as the Big Data of tomorrow because technologies keep changing. In short, it is relative.

The Kind of Data We Are Talking About

Organizations have a tradition of capturing transactional data. Besides that, organizations capture and store extra data from its operational environment at a fast speed. Some examples include:

- *Text data.* This is one of the biggest and most popular types of Big Data. The goal is all about developing major facts from a text and using the facts as inputs to remaining analytic process.

- *Web data.* The data from Web users such as searches, reading, page views, and purchasing can be captured. This can be used to improve performance in fields such as churn modeling, targeted advertisement, and customer segmentation.

- *Smart grid and sensor data.* Nowadays, sensor data is recorded from oil pipes, cars, and windmill turbines. This data is collected in an extremely higher frequency. The sensor data generates in-depth information related to the performance of machinery and engines. It facilitates the diagnosis of problems and faster development of mitigation mechanisms.

- *Time and location data.* The GPS, WI-FI connections, and mobile phones make time and location a good source of data. As a result, most organizations have come to understand the importance of monitoring the movements of their customers. The organizations embrace the need to know where their customers are at any given time. Another important thing is being able to look at time and location data at an aggregate level. While more individuals continue to open their location data and time, many good applications arise. Therefore, time and location data becomes one of the most privacy-sensitive Big Data types that must be treated with caution.

- *Social network data.* Within the social network sites such as Facebook, Instagram, and LinkedIn, it is possible for one to perform link analysis and discover the network of a given user. Social network analysis can present insights into what type of advertisements can appeal to users. This is achieved by taking into consideration the interests of customers and their circle of friends.

With many of these Big Data sources, the advantage doesn't lie in the type of data source but the value that it can generate in combination with other data sources. It is the combination that is very important.

The Difference between Big Data and the Traditional Data Sources

There are several ways in which Big Data differs from traditional data sources. First, Big Data can be viewed as a new data source. The type of transactions carried out isn't that different from transactions that would have been traditionally implemented. An organization can record Web transactions, but it will not be different from the transactions recorded a few years ago. The only difference comes to the behavior captured. The behavior may include browser behavior which then represents a form of new data.

Secondly, one can also argue that the speed of data has increased to the point where it merits to be considered as a new data source. For instance, the power meter used to be manually read. Nowadays, there is a smart meter that can automatically read power after ten minutes. One can further argue that frequency has increased to the point where it supports a different in-depth level of analysis.

Another difference between Big Data and traditional data is that there is an increase in semi-structured and unstructured data. The majority of the traditional sources fall in the structured realm. Structured data include receipts from the grocery store, data in the salary slip, accounting details on the spreadsheet, and any other thing that can be entered in a relational database. Each piece of information provided arrives in a specific format and particular order. This makes it very easy to handle.

Unstructured sources of data include that which one doesn't have any control over its format. Video data, text data, and audio data belong to this category. Unstructured data is very difficult to deal with because the meaning of bits and bytes is not predefined.

In the midst of structured and unstructured data, there lies semi-structured data. This is the type of data that is irregular and incomplete. In addition, its structure changes rapidly and unpredictably. In general, it has a structure, but it does not fit a fixed schema. Weblogs is a great example of semi-structured data.

It is necessary for an individual to work with Big Data rather than traditional data. If you read a lot of content that seems to hype Big Data, it is easy to think that simply because Big Data has a high volume, variety, and velocity, it is actually better than data. Well, this is not the case. The power of Big Data lies in the analysis and actions you take after the results of the analysis are out. Big Data by itself does not have any value. It is critical when you receive some insight about the data. And this kind of insight can be used to make a decision.

The Different Types of Insight

Besides data, there is something called paradigm shift based on the analytic focus. This refers to a change from descriptive analytics to predictive and prescriptive analytics. When it comes to descriptive analytics, it attempts to respond to questions about what happened in the past. Typically, this is all about reporting. Below are some examples of questions that are dealt with in descriptive analytics:

- Which is the most profitable customer or product?
- What amount of sales revenue was generated in the first quarter of the year?
- How many customers did we lose or win in the first half-year?
- How many customers did we win as a result of the promotional campaigns?

Predictive analytics focuses on something that may happen next. This is very difficult, and it involves extending trends and patterns of the future. Examples of questions include:

- What is the approximated number of a call center in the next quarter?
- What is the next best offer for this customer?
- Which customers are likely to churn?

The prescriptive analysis attempts to respond to questions related to "how can I handle this?" This is the point when analytics becomes operational. It is entirely business and case dependent. Some of the examples to demonstrate the point include:

- Knowing that an individual has a higher chance to churn, so he or she is presented with a value package.
- Determining the viewing history of a customer on the Web, then suggesting articles that the customer can read next.

All the above examples existed before Big Data. However, the major focus was entirely on reporting. But with the arrival of Big Data, it is now possible to:

- Derive a forward-looking insight.
- Increase the appetite and ability for quick and actionable insight.

A forward-looking insight means that a business could predict what may happen next. Traditionally, this was possible, but the accuracy was very limited.

Therefore, Big Data changed this equation. A fast and actionable insight meant that no matter what is derived from the data analysis, it has to have an effect on the business process and the embedded process.

For instance, a recommendation system can automatically generate personalized recommendations like the way Amazon recommends one to buy a different thing from what another person wants to buy because of the difference in viewing history. This doesn't mean that descriptive analytics is not that important. In fact, reporting will continue to be an important element in business life. In practice, it is advised that an individual should be flexible and apply different analytics – what will deliver the best results depends on the nature of the questions created and picking the correct tool for the right job.

Business Value of Big Data Analytics

Big Data delivers a significant benefit to any business. It helps draw insights from data, make smart decisions depending on the insight, and automate decisions.

In a detailed level, every Big Data solution addresses a specific problem that exists in organizations. As a result, when developing a business case that should be applied in a Big Data Analytics project, one should begin with a business problem instead of technology or data. Choosing to collect data or buy a given technology without having a clear business target is a wrong strategy.

The New Web: Visual, Semantic and API-POWERED

Since the introduction of the new Web, the Web has greatly changed. The Web as of today has become even more visual.

To upload a photo on the Web is just a click of a button. But this was not the case 20 years ago. If you can go back to the 1990s and think about how computers and the internet were then, you will realize how much effort has been made to improve and redefine technology.

Linked Data and Semantic Web

It is not just that data has increased in size alone, but also the Web grows, and data silos continue to reduce. Data has also continued to be interconnected. As of today, we are not close to connecting all the data. Most data sets cannot be easily connected to each other. However, major steps have been achieved now. The Web has continued to become more semantic.

Linked data refers to the practice of sharing, exposing, and integrating pieces of data, knowledge, and information on the same semantic Web. Both computing devices and human beings gain when data that is unconnected is connected. This is normally done through Web technologies such as uniform resource identifiers and Resource Description Framework.

The Ease of Accessing Data

Yes, there is a lot of data, more than what you can imagine, and most organizations have a challenge when it comes to drawing important insight from the data. Luckily, all hope is not lost. The available data management tools in organizations have never been so good and effective than today.

Before the internet era, many large organizations transferred their data from many different databases, systems, and data warehouses. Database experts and administrators created scripts and stored procedures which automated most of these processes. Batch procedures would run early in the morning.

Better Efficiency in the Clouds

It is true that Web cloud is causing a big impact in many organizations across the globe. The history of the Web started as the mainframe era before it went to the client-server era, and now we are in the mobile-cloud computing era. To move from one era to another called for a lot of developments and effort – this doesn't happen overnight.

The dawn of Big Data and Open Data created a lot of opportunities and room for organizations to enhance their operations. As a result, there has been a huge improvement in Business Intelligence solutions and statistical packages.

Level of Measurement

A decision tree can accommodate both quantitative and qualitative data. Quantitative data consists of weight and height. It describes quantities that one can modify using arithmetic operations such as subtraction, multiplication, and addition. On the other hand, qualitative may consist of gender and cannot be applied in arithmetic operations, but it is presented in decision trees.

Other types of data such as shoe size may both be quantitative and qualitative. For instance, you may fail to perform a meaningful arithmetic with shoe size although the number sequence in shoe size is in order.

Chapter 8: Data Science Tools Towards Data Science

There are a lot of Big Data tools that one can use for analysis. In simple terms, data analysis is defined as a process of inspecting, cleaning, transforming and modeling data with the sole reason to discover important information, conclusions and suggest the right decision. This chapter will outline to you the best tools which Data Scientists use in the process of cleaning, modeling, transforming, and analyzing data.

Open Source Data Tools

1. OpenRefine

This was formally called Google Refine. It is a great tool to use to work with data that is disorganized. This tool lets a Data Scientist clean and change the format of data. Additionally, a Data Scientist can decide to integrate the data with external data. The tool helps an individual perform large-scale data exploration and discover patterns in data easily.

2. Orange

An open source data visualization and analysis tool designed to be used by those people who are not experts in Data Science. It has a simple interactive workflow and an advanced toolbox to help a person build an interactive workflow that they can analyze and visualize data. However, the type of visualization which Orange creates is different from scatter plots, bar charts, and dendrograms.

3. Knime

KNIME is another open source solution to use in data analysis. This tool allows an individual to explore and discover hidden insights in data. The tool has over 1000 modules and hundreds of examples that one can run to learn how to use it. In addition, there is an advanced range of integrated tools and complex algorithms. KNIME offers some of the best toolboxes that any Data Scientist can use.

4. R-Programming

This is considered as the standard tool among statistical programming languages. Some people consider it the "golden boy" of Data Science. R is also open source software that anyone can install and use in statistical computing and graphics. It is compatible with Windows, MacOS platforms, and UNIX. It is useful in Data Science, and it has many job opportunities if you are an expert.

Since R is free, anybody can install it, use it, upgrade it, modify it, clone it and resell it. R will help one to save money on technological projects and offer regular updates that are useful for any statistical programming language. It is a high-performance language that will help users deal with an extensive data package and build a great tool to help manage Big Data. Also, it is best to use for resource-intensive applications.

Apart from Data Mining, using the R programming gives you the chance to apply a statistical and graphical technique. This includes linear and nonlinear modeling, time-series analysis, classical statistical tests, and clustering among many other methods.

5. RapidMiner

Similar to KNIME, RapidMiner deals with visual programming and is the best when it comes to modeling, analyzing, and manipulation of data. RapidMiner improves the productivity of Data Science teams. It has an open-source platform to support Machine Learning, model deployment, and data preparation. Since it is an integrated Data Science platform, it speeds the development of a complete analytical workflow from model validation, Machine Learning, and deployment.

6. Pentaho

Pentaho deals with problems that affect the ability of an organization to accept value from different data. The platform will simplify data preparation and data blending as well as a collection of tools used in the analysis, visualization, reporting, exploration, and prediction. Pentaho is designed to ensure that each member of a team can transform data into value.

7. Weka

Another open source software designed with the capability to handle Machine Learning algorithms to use in Data Mining tasks. You can directly use the algorithm to process a data set. It is also the best to use in developing a new Machine Learning scheme because it is implemented fully in the JAVA programming.

Since the Graphical User Interface of Weka is simple and easy to use, it facilitates an easy transition into the field of data science. Written in the Java language, anyone experienced in Java can invoke the library into their code.

8. The NodeXL

A data visualization and analysis tool that shows relationships in a data set. Since it is open-source software, it is free to use to analyze and create visualizations from data. It is one of the best tools in Statistics that you can use to analyze data. It has different modules such as social network data importers and automation. With NodeXL, you will still analyze your data fast and easy.

9. Gelphi

Written in Java language, Gelphi comes as an open-source visualization and network analysis tool.

10. Talend

It is the leading open source integration software provider to most data-driven enterprises. Talend allows customers from any place to connect easily.

Data Visualization

11. Datawrapper

It is an online data-visualization software that one can use to build interactive charts. A user will upload data from CSV, Excel or PDF files into the field. This tool processes the data and generates a map, bar, and line. Graphs produced by Datawrapper can be installed into any website that is built with ready to use embed codes.

12. Tableau Public

This tool will democratize visualization in a very elegant and simple way. It is a very powerful tool to use in any type of business. One can identify data insights with the help of Tableau data visualization tools. When it comes to analytics, visualization in Tableau allows a Data Scientist to explore data before moving into a complex statistical process.

13. Infogram

It has over 35 interactive charts and over 500 maps to allow an individual to visualize data in the most beautiful way. It creates different charts such as word cloud, pie, and bar. Infogram also supports a map module that can capture the attention of the audience.

14. Google Fusion Tables

This is one of the most interesting and powerful data analysis tools. It is the best to use when you have a large data set that you want to visualize and map. With its powerful mapping software, Google plays an important role in creating this tool.

15. Solver

This is built with the ability to support effective financial reporting, budgeting and analysis. It has a push-button that will let anyone to access and interact with data that generates more profit in a company.

Sentiment Tools

16. OpenText

This is a specialized classification engine applied in the identification and evaluation of expressions and patterns in a textual content. The analysis takes place at the document, sentence, and topic level.

17. Trackur

An automated sentiment analysis software which highlights a particular keyword tracked by an individual. Trackur has an algorithm which monitors all social media and mainstream news to draw important insights through the discovery of trends.

18. Opinion Crawl

Another online sentiment analysis software applied in the analysis of the latest news, products, and companies. It gives freedom to every visitor to access Web sentiment in a specific topic. Anyone can type, participate in a topic, and receive ad-hoc sentiment assessment. For each topic, there is a pie chart to display the latest real-time sentiment and a list of current news headlines. Besides that, there are different thumbnail images and a cloud tag to include different concepts that the public can easily relate with. This tool allows a person to see events which affect the sentiment positively or negatively. To create a comprehensive analysis, Web crawlers search for the latest content published on common subjects and current public issues.

Data Extraction Tools

19. Content Grabber

This is a tool designed for enterprises. The tool is built with the function to support content mining from any website and save that in a structured format. This consists of CSV, XML, and Excel reports. It is the best tool for an expert at programming because it has scripting and editing module. Also, users can still use C#, VB.NET to debug and write script information to take of the crawling process.

20. IBM Cognos Analytics

Before this tool was developed, Cognos Business Intelligence was the one used. It is designed with a Web-based interface to support data visualization in the BI product. It has modules for data governance, self-service analytics, and management. This tool also supports the integration of data from different source to create reports and visualizations.

21. Sage Live

This is a cloud-based accounting platform that supports both small and mid-sized types of businesses. It allows the creation of invoices, payment of bills, and sales using a mobile device. Furthermore, if you want a data visualization tool that supports different companies, currencies, and banks, then this could be the right tool to use.

22. Gawk

GNU lets one use a computer without software. A gawk is a tool that can interpret unique programming language. It helps users handle simple-data reformatting jobs by writing down a few lines of code. It has the following main features:

- It is data driven instead of procedural
- Makes it easy for one to read and write programs
- Searches for lines and other text units that have one or more patterns

23. GraphLab Create

Both Data Scientists and developers use this tool to build state-of-the-art data products using Machine Learning. This type of machine modeling tool will help users create smart applications. The major features of this tool include:

- Integrates automatic feature engineering, Machine Learning visualizations, and model selection to the application.
- Identifies and links records both within and across data sources that have the same real-world entity.
- It simplifies the development of Machine Learning models.

24. Netlink Business Analytics

It is one of the most comprehensive on-demand solutions. You can access it through a Web browser or any other device and apply it in a full enterprise. You can share the dashboards among teams using collaboration features. Most of the features are tailored towards sales and complicated analytic capability based on inventory forecasting, fraud detection, sentiment, and customer churn analysis.

25. Apache Spark

The tool is designed to run-in memory and real time. As a result, it facilitates faster real-time analytics.

The Top 5 Data Analytics Tools and Techniques

1. Visual analytics

There are different methods that one can use to analyze data. For instance, by building a graph and discovering unique spots. This method consists of other methods such as human interaction, data analysis, and visualization.

2. Business Experiments

AB testing, business experiments, and the experimental design consist of all techniques applied in testing the validity of something.

3. Regression Analysis

This method will allow you to identify a relationship between two different variables and the strength of the relationship.

4. Correlation Analysis

This is a statistical technique which will let you identify whether a relationship exists between two different variables. This method is perfect when you have some suspicion that there is a special relationship between the two variables.

5. Time series analysis

Here, data is gathered at uniform time intervals. You can use it any time you want to identify changes and predict future events depending on what has happened in the past.

Chapter 9: Data Security – Protect Major Enterprise Assets

A Security Data Scientist refers to a specialist in data analysts for fraud and security. They have a different range of specialties which might consist of one or more of the following:

- Security metrics
- Malware analysis
- Insider threat detection
- Fraud and loss analytics
- Computer and network forensics
- And many more

Security Data Science

This phrase refers to the application of complicated analytics to access and discover unknown risks. In general, Data Science refers to the method of extracting important insights from data.

When it comes to security, important data insights help reduce risks. Data Science has emerged to fulfill the challenges of processing extensive data sets, "Big Data", and the exploration of new data produced by smart devices, social media, and the Web. Data science has a long and rich history of fraud and security. Both information security and fraud monitoring fields have been going through changes to deal with problems and draw insights from extensive data.

Why Security Data Science?

This is focused on upgrading information security via practical applications of Statistics, Data Analysis, Machine Learning, and Data Visualization. While the tools and techniques are not different compared to those applied in Data Science, this field has a major focus on decreasing risk and identification of fraud.

It is believed that domain knowledge and experience is important in the successful application of analytics to cut down on the risk and fraud losses.

Unmasking Information Security Using Data Science

It is not easy to find good resources written about security Data Science on the Web.

What is the Reason for Increased Ransomware Attacks and Data Breaches?

There are quite a number of reasons to explain the rise in ransomware attacks and data breaches:

- Attackers discover an efficient way to generate quick cash using ransomware. One reason for this is that you can find ransomware as a service on the dark Web. As a result, attackers can choose to leverage on the ransomware service and concentrate on the ransom extortion.

- The attack surface has increased, and the network perimeter is dissolved as a result of cloud and mobile.

- Attackers have increased the number of tools as a means to escape the current information security tools.

- The information security team has insufficient cameras to monitor movements of an intruder in the network enterprise. Therefore, adversaries have an advantage because they can move in any direction within the network of an enterprise.

Challenges of Information Security

- There are many points of vulnerability that an attacker can use to enter into a network enterprise. It is not easy to provide total security because the tools that you use to enforce security of a network aren't 100% perfect. Some may fail to distinguish between a genuine user and intruder.

- Information security is skewed. The security team has a responsibility to write down more than 10,000 lines of code to fix a point of intrusion and enforce system security. However, adversaries just need to identify a point of weakness to attack and create a security patch.

- The adversaries apply the same commands, tools, and scripts that system administrators use. Based on the skillset of the attacker, they can choose to use a tool such as Nmap, Metasploit, and PowerSploit.

Why Information Security Should Have a Data Scientist

Once attackers get close to an enterprise network, they need to determine the point at which they are. Once they identify the locations, they approach the targets and perform the attack. While carrying out some of these operations, they may leave behind certain traces to reveal their signals. These signals can be found in data, and their presence can be unearthed with the help of a Data Scientist.

In the beginning, all the data used to be transferred to a security data lake such as Security Information and management (SIEM). However, with the availability of complex Data Science techniques, associations across many events could be carried out in real time. By using algorithms, it is possible to connect dots and discover patterns.

One advantage that comes with Data Science is that it learns from decisions executed by security analysts. Once the system has been trained completely, it starts to execute similar preventive measures done by security analysts automatically.

Challenges of Data Science in the Information Security

Challenges experienced in information security are multi-dimensional. What this means is that many features exist in tons of data sources. That is why it is critical to identify the presence of an attacker through mining data found in machine logs. This is one of the most complex problems because both the signal to noise ratio is very low. In addition, to set up a link between independent and attack sequences is a very big endeavor.

Most of the security data does not have labels, and this makes it even difficult to use Deep Learning networks in a large number of information security cases.

But the industry has chosen to deal with this problem by producing class labels. For instance, detection of malware and ranking of DNS domains is completely done by application of Machine Learning techniques.

Another way these cases are applied in security Data Science is in the development of a baseline for every network, then making comparisons to discover anomalies.

Major Data Sources and Use Cases

The information security has an extensive number of logs. Both the volume of data and variety depends on the organization's size and domain. Below is a list of a typical data source for information security:

Endpoints: Applications, processes, host-based IDS alerts, registry changes, operating system logs, file system changes, and anti-virus alerts.

Threat Intelligence: These indicate whether a system is compromised.

Vulnerability Logs

Network: Network packets and flows, network topology, firewall logs, DNS logs, Bro logs, and HTTP proxy logs.

Asset Management Logs

Majority of the above logs show visibility related to the adversary's presence and activities.

The Evolution of Security Data Science

The security Data Science has undergone the evolution of three phases:

1. Rule-based and Detection of An Anomaly By Systems

Data Science has been playing an important role, especially in information security. This started with rule-based techniques that helped an individual discover strange activities in the intrusion detection system and prevention.

Rules are defined and set up by security experts. In case of an intrusion, an alert is sent out. For instance, if an attacker tries to break into a system and reaches the maximum count of attempts, an alert is sent out to the security experts.

These anomaly detection systems usually depend on the normal behavior of network and hosts. This means that when something extends beyond the normal behavior, an alert is generated. Fortunately, there are anomaly detection algorithms to detect any unusual activity.

Anomaly-based algorithms are built on networks to facilitate:

- Hosts and users that have abnormal behavior
- Excessive DNS failures
- Anomalous ports
- Unusual traffic from a host

However, many of the AD systems generated false alarms and call for security analysts to confirm the alerts.

2. Security Data Lakes

It is important to transfer an alert and combine multiple data sources in the security data lake.

3. Malware Detection

Big Data frameworks have a new security Data Science technique. This makes it possible to use row logs in real time and generates alerts. As a result, new user and entity behavior have been created to leverage on Spark and detection of an anomaly. So far, enterprises can quickly notice when there is an inside attack because of the new solutions invented. However, there are still some issues with the same means to detect an anomaly.

Another area that has increasingly gained attention is the endpoint security where there is Deep Learning applied in the detection and classification of malware. Supervised ML algorithms are applied in the classification of malicious scripts, detection of DNS tunnels, malware detection, application of attacks, and a lot of known threats that include labels present in the training system.

4. Deception-triggered Data Science

In the modern world, a new paradigm shift for information security field has evolved. In the security defense, deception is applied first in the entire enterprise network. Next, Data Science is used to profile the behavior of an adversary and their actions in the network.

Deception triggered Data Science is not the same with normal data security Data Science. For the normal data security, it mainly depends on techniques to detect a glitch in network traffic. Even if this method starts with a real attack, a glitch revealed by a deception activity does not need an anomaly detection algorithm.

Deception alerts represent a critical alert. Data Science is similar to other security events which have a high-fidelity alert to draw insights related to the adversary behavior. In this situation, context is collected and described around a deception alert rather than searching for anomalies. This type of Data Science can dwell most on capturing everything that is linked to an attack.

Three Trends in Security Data Science in 2018

1. Machine Learning for Response Automation

Machine Learning has proven to be an important tool when it comes to detecting evidence of threats used in compiling a report. Security experts can subconsciously train themselves to respond to evidence of an event in a given way. The key to information security depends on the information security analysts plus a majority of the knee-jerk responses that can be automated. In most cases, the response may be Machine Learning automated.

The information overload pain is not a recent problem for Machine Learning. However, various pressures call for a more widespread application of ML to simplify a response via Machine Learning distillation instead of complex additional evidence. Some of them include:

- Market pressure to maximize workflows
- Diminishing returns on reduction time

Actions to Take

- Identify remediation workflows of security analysts in the organization.
    1. What evidence associated with the incident indicates a high confidence to respond?
    2. What evidence shows how to respond?
    3. For a typical event, how many decisions need to be made during remediation?
    4. What tasks could be automated?
    5. At the moment, what is being automated?
- Don't force a solution on security analysts.

- Review how existing solutions can automate and simplify remediation steps.

2. Machine Learning to Handle Automation

There have been trials to reveal how AI can scale digital attacks. Toolsets are making the barrier to entry low. There are several economic drivers to facilitate bypassing of CAPTCHA. The current security risks and exploits are much more embarrassing and complex for advanced adversaries to succeed.

Actions to do

- Protect users using more than simple CAPTCHA codes and simple image techniques that human beings can solve trivially.
- Be ready for unlikely incidents.
- Stay familiar with pen testing and red-teaming tools.

3. Model compliance

Global laws determine the design, engineering, and operational costs of security Data Science solutions. The laws provide strict guidelines on the handling of data, movement, and model-building constraints. Model compliance is not a one-time investment. Privacy laws can change depending on the political landscape.

Creating models which adhere to compliance laws is critical. Some of the actions which you can do include:

- End customers should audit data and tag it correctly.
- Perform tiered modeling: Every geographic region should be modeled separately, and then the results need to be scrubbed and transferred to a global model.

The Value of Data Science in Security

Data Science is a major organ in security. To realize Big Data and opportunities presented by Data Science, it is important to ensure that technologies and infrastructure on which a system operates should be trusted. Security is an important element in the future of Big Data. Data Science is another important tool that can help security organizations realize success in this domain.

A popularly cited example of Data Science for security purposes comes from the banking and insurance industry. In these fields, Data Science creates a combination of analytics and Machine Learning to determine false transactions.

By reviewing data sets associated with network behavior, companies can identify mistakes and generate an alert. This basic technique can be deployed to work for security applications. The applications help determine intrusion on a company network as well as discover users who go against corporate policies and task management.

With the presence of Machine Learning, both algorithms and models can now be improved to reflect changes in staff behavior, and changes in technology to help reduce the increasing number of unnecessary alerts that staff is called to respond to. As with any other Data Science project, professionals in security can only advance when they have the correct data. However, with the decreasing cost of storing data and the ease of collecting data, businesses can find themselves collecting a lot of information and holding to it as long as they want.

When it comes to security, a lot of data makes it hard to validate use in cases for Data Science. Even though it is difficult to carry out predictive analytics, Data Science for security trends must be more focused. When looking for patterns and anomalies, it might be profitable to carry out on a smaller data sample. But until now, how Data Science is used in information security remains a puzzle.

Chapter 10: Mastering Your Data with Probability

It is hard to be a Data Scientist without having knowledge of probability. All Data Scientist experts have a good knowledge of probability and mathematics.

It is worthy to think of probability as a means of validating the uncertainty linked with events selected from a certain universe of events. Instead of mastering the technical terms of probabilities, imagine rolling a dice. The universe is made up of all outcomes. Any subset of the following results is an event. For example, "the die rolls a four" or "the die rolls an odd number".

The mathematical notation for probability is P (E) to refer to "the probability of the event E".

The probability theory helps one to build models. In this chapter, you will learn how probability theory is used to examine models.

Dependence and Independence

Basically, two events E and F are said to be dependent if by having knowledge about whether E takes place generates information about whether F happens. If not, then it is said to be independent.

For example, if you flip a two-sided coin twice and the first flip is a Head, it does not mean that on the second flip you will get a Head. In other words, these two events are independent. Conversely, if by flipping the first event generates information to help us determine the outcome of the second event, then both events are said to be dependent.

In mathematics, events E and F are said to be independent if the probability that both take place is the product of probabilities of each one happening.

$$P(E, F) = P(E) P(F)$$

In the example of tossing a coin, the probability of the first flip is 0.5, and the probability of both flips is 0.25. However, as you can imagine, if there's two flips being made, the probability of the first toss being a Head, and both flips being Tails is 0.

Conditional Probability

When two events E and F are independent, then it is defined as:

$$P(E, F) = P(E) P(F)$$

In case they aren't independent, and the probability of F is not zero, then the probability of E is said to be conditional on F:

$$P(E/F) = P(E, F) / P(F)$$

This can be paraphrased as the probability of E taking place given that F happens.

This can be rewritten as:

$$P(E, F) = P(E/F) P(F)$$

If E and F are independent, then you can move on to confirm:

$$P(E/F) = P(E)$$

This is a mathematical expression which means that having knowledge about the occurrence of F does not provide extra information about the occurrence of E.

A popular example to explain this concept is the family with two unknown children.

If that is the assumption, then:

1. Every child is equally likely to be a girl or boy.

2. The gender of the second child does not depend on the gender of the first child.

Therefore, the event "no girls" will have the probability of 0.25, the event "one girl, one boy" will have the probability of 0.5., and finally the event "two girls" will have the probability 0.25. So you can move on and find out the probability of "both children are girls" conditional on the event "the older child is a girl" by application of the conditional probability.

Bayes' Theorem

It is one of the best theorems for Data Scientists. Bayes' theorem involves reversing conditional probabilities. Take for instance when you want to figure out the probability of event E conditional on another event F happening. However, the only information available is the probability of F conditional on E occurring.

The Bayes' theorem is usually used to show why Data Scientists are more intelligent than doctors. For example, a specific disease affects 1 out of 10,000 people. Imagine that there is a test for this particular disease which displays the correct result "diseased" in case you have the disease and "no diseased" if you don't have the disease 99% of the time.

So, what will a positive test show? According to Bayes's theorem, the probability that you have the disease, conditional on testing positive, is 0.98%. As you can see, this is less than 1% of the people who test positive. While Bayes' theorem presents us with this result, many doctors will approximate it as 2%.

Another way you can look at this is by imagining a population made up of 1 million people. You might expect 100 of them to have the disease and 99 out of those 100 people to test positive. Conversely, you may expect 999,900 of them to be free of the disease, while 9,999 to test positive. In other words, you will expect only 99 from (99 + 9999) positive testers to have the disease.

Random Variables

A random variable describes a variable whose positive value is associated with the probability distribution. A simple random variable is equivalent to 1 if tossing a coin shows Heads and 0 if the tossing displays a Tail. An advanced one may count the number of Heads recorded when flipping a coin ten times or a value selected from a range (10) where each number is equally likely.

The similarity in the distribution shows the probabilities that the variable achieves each of its prospective values. The variable after tossing a coin equals 0 with a probability of 0.5 and 1 having a probability of 0.5. The range of (10) variable contains a distribution which allocates a probability 0.1 to every number from 0 to 9.

There is an aspect called expected value of a random variable that you will soon learn. This is the average of its values weighted by their probabilities. The tossing of a coin variable has an expected value of 1/2 (= 0 * 1/2 + 1 * 1/2), and the range (10) variable contains an expected value of 4.5. Besides this, one can condition random variables on events similar to other events.

Continuous Distributions

Tossing a coin is equivalent to a discrete distribution. In this case, a positive probability is linked with discrete outcomes. Usually, an individual might want to model distributions across a continuum of outcomes. For instance, the uniform distribution assigns equal weight on all numbers between 0 and 1.

Since there are many numbers between 0 and 1, this implies that the weight it allocates to individual points should be zero.

Normal Distribution

This is the king of all distributions. It is the classic bell curved-shaped distribution determined by two parameters: mean and standard deviation. Mean will display the location where the bell is centered while standard deviation illustrates how wide it is.

The Central Limit Theorem

When you have a lot of data to work with, you might find it hard to decide the method to use to retrieve meaningful information from it. In fact, it is very hard to tell what is going on underneath the data. To deal with this problem, a small amount of data is extracted and studied. However, a small chunk of data is not satisfactory. It is important to take a look at multiple chunks to increase confidence in the results.

Let's assume that you have the level of cholesterol of people from country A. Then it is possible to determine the mean, median, and mode of the data. You can plot a histogram that contains meaningful ranges and review the data. Assume that the data resembles the figure shown below. The mean of the following data is 153.2.

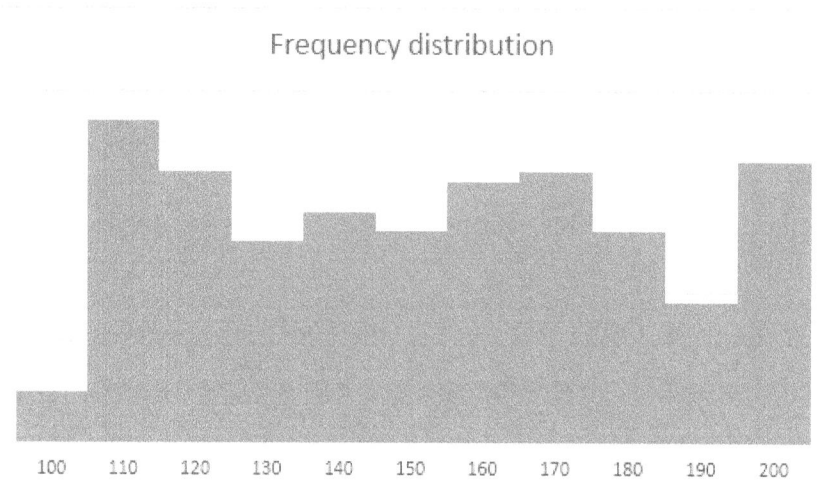

This is an extensive data that is going to be very difficult to process. To process the data, data of 50 people is extracted and used to calculate the mean.

Next, another sample of 50 people is taken and used to calculate the mean. This is done several times before the mean of these samples is plotted.

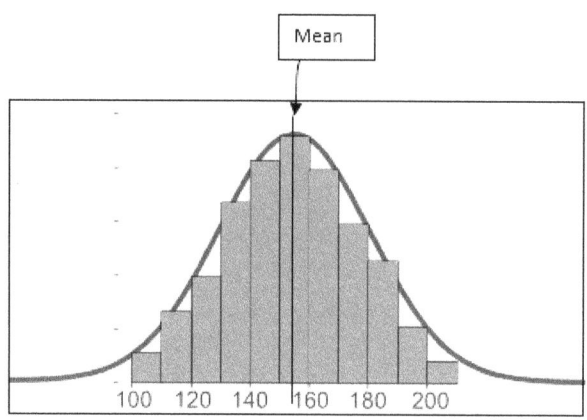

As you can see, the above sample means to create a frequency distribution that appears symmetrical. The frequency close to the original data is the highest and reduces once you move farther from the mean. This implies that if we extract cholesterol levels of 50 people and calculate the mean, it will range from 150 to 160. Only a few mean values will go past 170 and be lower than 140.

Normal Distribution

Earlier, it was referred to as a bell curve. It appears like this:

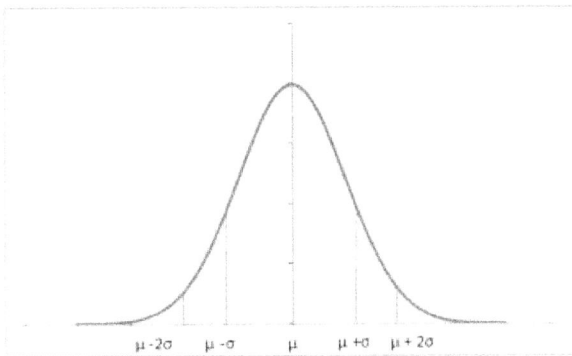

A normal distribution is perfectly symmetrical to the mean. Probabilities in a normal distribution move the same direction as the mean. The area under the curve is 1 and adding all the possible probabilities will result in 1.

This type of distribution can change depending on how data is spread. If the data has a high range and standard deviation, the normally distributed curve spreads out and flatters.

Apart from this, the majority of the values don't lie close to the mean. Therefore, the probability of data being close to the mean decreases. Again, if the standard deviation is low, it means that the values will be close to the mean. So, there is a higher chance for the sample mean to be close to the mean. Remember: the higher the standard deviation, the bigger and flatter the curve gets.

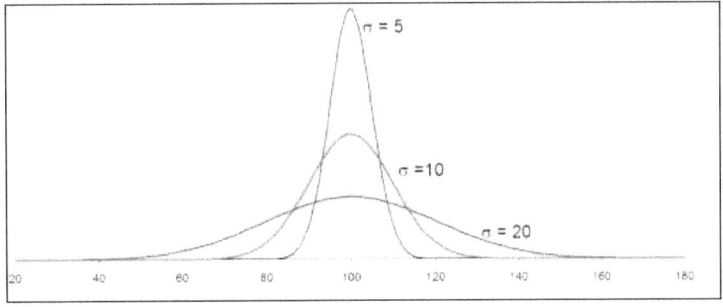

Below are the Main Points:

- There is an extensive probability for means to get close to the actual mean of the data instead of being far away.

- The area of the probability density function represents the probability of a random variable in that range.

- Normal distributions large standard deviation expands compared to lower standard deviations.

Area in the Normal Distribution

Assume that you have a cholesterol data set of various patients and you would like to determine the probability of healthy patients. The mean value (μ) for all patients' cholesterol is equivalent to 150, and the standard deviation is equivalent to 15.

Can you see that patients who are healthy are one standard deviation on either side of the mean? This means that you have to compute the area under the curve letting 135 and 165 as the limits.

This particular area for normal distribution has been calculated, and the percentage is 68%.

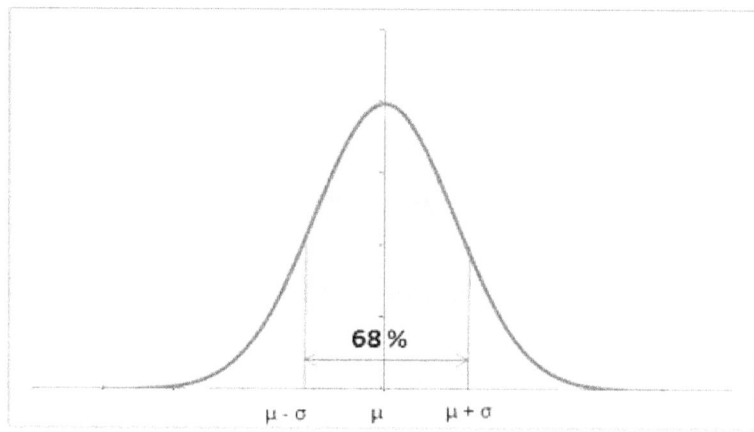

Z scores

In Statistics, there are many cases where the probability will be less or more than a particular value. This value won't equal 1σ or 2σ as the distance from the mean. Z score is the distance that depends on the number of standard deviations and observed value from the mean.

When you have a positive z score, the observed value is Z standard deviations more than the mean. On the other hand, a negative Z score means that the value is below the mean.

Observed value = $\mu + z\sigma$ while μ is the mean and σ represents the standard deviation.

Chapter 11: Data in the Cloud

Data Science refers to an intersection of many important concepts.

To be a Data Scientist, you need to have solid programming skills. Even though you might not be familiar with all programming concepts, such as general production software architecture and infrastructure, you are required to have some basic skills in computer science concepts. Before you start a Data Science class, it is a must that you install R language and Python on your computer.

While advanced analytics continues to expand, Data Science teams continue to evolve. This calls for a collaborative solution such as a recommendation system, predictive analytics and so on. Research and notebook tools integrated with code source control are an example of a collaboration solution.

Collaborative requires inclusion of those working outside especially when Data Science sets out to accomplish business goals.

What is a Cloud?

While it sounds hypothetical and abstract, a cloud has a concrete meaning. Before moving on, here are some definitions of a few concepts that you need to know:

Network. This refers to a collection of computers connected together that share resources. The internet is a good example of a network. Home networks like Wi-Fi Service Set and Local Area Network have multiple computers connected. Shared resources include media, web pages, app servers, data storage, and printers.

Computers in a network are referred to as **nodes.** Intercommunication between computers is through internet protocols such as HTTP, TCP, and IP. Some of these communication protocols can help update a status, make a request, and many other uses.

Additionally, it is hard for computers to be located on premise. In other words, both data and applications are found on computers in the data center. A data center is useful because it has the necessary infrastructure to support security and protection among others.

Since the cost of computers and storage has continued to reduce over time, many solutions now involve multiple computers that work together, and they aren't that costly when one wants to scale. This is very different from scaling solutions which include buying a powerful and expensive computing device. The reason for collaboration is to facilitate continuous operation even if a single computer breaks down. Besides this, collaboration enhances the system so that it can automatically scale and handle any load that is applied.

Popular social networking sites such as YouTube, Netflix, and Facebook are good examples of cloud applications that must be scaled. It is rare to see these applications failing. This is because they have their systems hosted in the cloud.

A **cluster** refers to a group of computers connected to the same network and all work to accomplish a similar task. You can consider it as a single computer that can improve performance, scalability, and availability.

Next, let's define the cloud. In simple terms, **cloud** refers to the process where a single entity can have total control over a group of network computers and generate software solutions. Depending on how the cloud is defined, the internet is said to be a network and not a cloud.

Data Science in the Cloud

Anyone who is familiar with Data Science is aware that the process takes place in the local machine of the Data Scientists. The computer is already installed with a programming language. This can be R or Python. The Data Scientist further installs relevant development packages using a manager such as Anaconda or installs individual packages manually.

Once the development environment is ready, then the usual Data Science workflow starts, with data as the only element needed.

Sometimes, it is not a must to carry out all the Data Science and Big Data related tasks in a different local development environment. Here are the reasons why:

- The development environment processing power fails to carry out tasks in a reasonable amount of time.

- Presence of large data sets that cannot be contained in the development environment's system memory.

- Deliverables must be arrayed into a production environment and incorporated as a component in a large application.

- It is advised to use a machine that is fast and powerful.

If such instances arise, there are many options to take. Instead of using a local environment of a Data Scientist, people deploy the computing task to an on-premise machine or even a cloud-based virtual machine. The advantages of using virtual machines and auto-scaling clusters are one can span up and discard it any time they need. Also, it is customized to fulfill one's computing power and storage needs.

The process of deploying a deliverable into a production environment so that it can be used in a large data pipeline has many challenges that an individual must consider.

Besides the custom developed cloud-based solutions, there are still many clouds and service-based offerings available from specific vendors.

Software Architecture and Quality Attributes

Software architects design a software system that is cloud-based. This system may represent a product, service or a task dependent on the computing system.

One of the tasks involved in building software architecture includes selecting the right language to program. This may call for much consideration, especially centered on the purpose of the system. This part of software architecture requires a person who is experienced and skilled.

Cloud computing enhances an agile culture. It is a mature market, and several large companies have started to build effective and elastic cloud environments. Some of these environments have been deployed on pools of server, networking resources, and storage. They are more cost-effective, and this seems to increase the ROI of advanced analytics.

Generally, applications built to support and use cloud embrace and allow fast-moving as well as enhance creativity from teams. Additionally, teams are taking advantage of the big space in the cloud to store more data and discover a lot of use cases for data. With cloud computing, it is possible to release a feature now and have it tested immediately to reveal whether it adds value.

Sharing Big Data in the Cloud

In the enterprise world, the role of Big Data cannot be ignored. Also, the cloud makes it easy to track and analyze insights. Once it is integrated, Big Data delivers value to all types of organizations.

Traditionally, it was risky to let business process wired data into silos. Teams had a big problem when they wanted to share insights. Collaboration used to be a big problem, not forgetting to mention the difficulty in transferring large amounts of data. Cloud computing has reduced most of these problems and made it easy for teams to work together across different distances.

It is very difficult to ignore the benefits of cloud computing in the Big Data field. In fact, most companies across the world rely on the cloud. Take Uber and Airbnb for example. These companies adopt cloud computing as a means to improve information sharing and data.

Getting Big Data Insights Fast Using Cloud

There was a time when Big Data was considered expensive and overwhelming. During this period, efforts in Big Data needed to be reactionary and generate insights.

Cloud computing removed the need of a data warehouse. This means that you don't need to worry about analyzing, compiling, and collecting data because you will have the best tools to use in Big Data.

Take the example of gathering customer analytics in Data Science. If you choose to use cloud and Big Data technology, it will make the whole process easy and allow you to collect information from various sources in sales, marketing, and web analytics.

Even without the need of massive servers, companies can get data and quickly analyze it before making use of it. They can do this by using Hadoop and other applications discussed in the other chapters. Whether large or small, companies can take advantage of Big Data by adopting cloud-based servers, software, and technologies. This will help reduce the cost of IT and increase flexibility and scalability.

Cloud and Big Data Governance

Cloud is a great thing, right? However, most companies are scared about how to regulate governance, privacy, and control. Big Data comes with its challenges, and implementation of cloud data brings with it issues on privacy and security.

This is the reason why it is critical to develop a solid governance plan in your cloud solutions. Make sure that it is an open architecture and forward compatible. This will ensure that your cloud solution remains robust and governable.

Why Do Data Scientists Need Cloud Tools to Deliver the Value of Data for Businesses?

Data Scientists help organizations to begin using data for transformative purposes. Data Scientists continue to be in great demand today because of the massive data that organizations have and need to deal with. There is about 80% of unstructured data that organizations receive in the form of social media, emails, videos, and images.

With the growth in cloud computing, Data Scientists need to deal with new workloads from IoT devices, AI, and analytics. Accessing data in the cloud is important to any Data Scientist today, and they require a centralized and accessible platform across all teams.

As digital growth continues to power many companies and industries around the world, there is an increasing need to record and manage new and legacy data.

Once a Data Scientist has easy access to this particular data, he or she is already equipped with the right skills to analyze the increasing volumes via cloud technology and turn information into insights which can change industries and businesses.

Most companies employ a Data Scientist to build an algorithm and Machine Learning model, which is part of their favorite job. Data Scientists spend about 80% searching, cleaning, and organizing data. This leaves only 20% to analyzing of the data.

As a result, organizations must create new cloud services and technology to enable Data Scientists with the tools needed to search and organize massive data quickly. This will set aside more time to concentrate on where their skills are most valuable. Such areas include analyzing and working with the growing data set generated by sensors and users. Cloud is the main ground that will allow Data Scientists to save, access, and extend models.

Chapter 12: Artificial Neural Networks

Machine Learning is a branch of computer science which powers the rapid development of Artificial Intelligence. Machine Learning will study an algorithm and let machines recognize patterns, develop models, and generate videos and images via learning. Machine Learning algorithms can be created using different methods such as clustering, decision trees, linear regression, and many more.

What is an Artificial Neural Network?

Artificial Neural Network is propelled by biological models of brain and biological neural networks. In brief, Artificial Neural Network (ANN) refers to a computational representation of the human neural network which alters human intelligence, memory, and reasoning. But why should the human brain system develop effective ML algorithms?

The major principle behind ANN is that neural networks are effective in advanced computations and hierarchical representation of knowledge. Dendrites and axons connect neurons into complex neural networks that can pass and exchange information as well as store intermediary computation results.

Therefore, a computational model of such systems can be effective in learning processes that resemble biological ones.

The perception algorithm created in 1957 was the trial to build a computational model of a biological neural network. However, advanced neural networks that have multiple layers, neurons, and nodes became possible just recently.

ANN is the reason for the recent success in computer vision and image recognition. Natural Language Processing and other applications of machine language seek to extract complex patterns from data. Neural networks are very useful when one wants to study nonlinear hypothesis that has many features. Building a precise hypothesis for a massive feature space may need one to have multiple high order polynomials that would inevitably result in overfitting. This is a situation where a model reveals random noise in data instead of the underlying patterns of relationships. The issue with overfitting involves image recognition problems. Here, each pixel represents a feature.

A Simple Neural Network That Has a Single Neuron

The simplest neural network has a single 'neuron' as shown below.

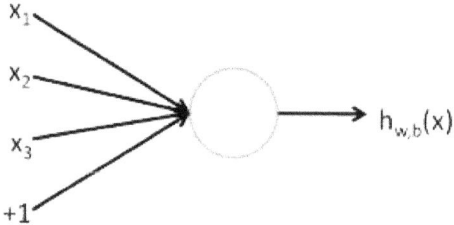

By applying a biological analogy, this neuron represents a computational unit that assumes inputs through electrical inputs and transfers them using axons to the next network output.

In the above simple neural network, dendrites refer to input features (x1, X2) and the output is the result of the hypothesis hw,b(x). Apart from the input features, the input layer of the neural network contains a bias unit that is equivalent to 1. A bias unit is required to apply a constant term in the function hypothesis.

In machine learning, the above network contains a single input layer, a hidden layer, and one output layer. To implement the learning process for this network, the input layer accepts input features for every training sample and feeds it to the activation function which computes the hypothesis in the hidden layer.

An activation function is a logistic regression applied in classification. However, other options are also possible. In the above case, a single neuron is similar to the input-output mapping defined by a logistic regression.

$$y = \varsigma(x) = \frac{1}{1+e^{-x}}$$

Multi-layered Neural Network

To understand how neural network operates, it is important to formalize the model and explain it in a real-world scenario. The image below represents a multilayer network that has three layers and various neurons. In this case, just like a single-neuron network, there is one input layer that has three inputs (x1, x2, x3) that has an added bias unit (+1). The second network layer is a hidden layer that has three units represented by activation functions. This is called a hidden layer because the values that are computed in it aren't observed. Basically, a neural network contains multiple hidden layers that pass advanced computations and functions from surface layers to the bottom of the neural network. The design of a neural network that has a lot of hidden layers is constantly used in Deep Learning.

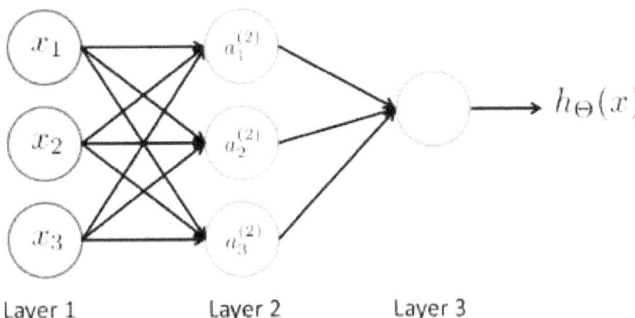

The hidden layer 2 has three neurons (a12, a22, a32). Each neuron of a hidden layer activates layer j. In this case, a unit a1 activates the first neuron of the second layer. Activation means that the value that is computed by function activation in this layer is output by the same node to the next layer.

Layer 3 is the output layer that receives results from the hidden layer and applies its own activation function. This layer calculates the final value of the hypothesis. Next, the cycle continues until that point when the neural network comes up with the model and weights which best predict the values of the training data.

Chapter 13: Data Science Modeling and Featurization

Data modeling is an important aspect of Data Science. It is one of the most rewarding processes that receive the most attention among learners of Data Science. However, things aren't the same as they might look because there is so much to it rather than applying a function to a given class of package.

The biggest part of Data Science is assessing a model to make sure that it is strong and reliable. In addition, Data Science modeling is highly associated with building information feature set. It involves different processes which make sure that the data at hand is harnessed in the best way.

Robust Data Model

Robust data models are important in creating the production. First, they must have better performance depending on different metrics. Usually, a single metric can mislead the way a model performs because there are many aspects in the classification problems.

Sensitivity analysis describes another important aspect of Data Science modeling. This is something that is important for testing a model to make sure it is strong. Sensitivity refers to a condition which the output of a model is meant to change considerably if the input changes slightly. This is very undesirable because it must be checked since the robust model is stable.

Lastly, interpretability is an essential aspect even though it is not always possible. This is usually related to how easy one can interpret the results of a model. But most modern models resemble black boxes. This makes it hard for one to interpret them. Besides that, it is better to go for an interpretable model because you might need to defend the output from others.

How Featurization Is Achieved

For a model to work best, it must require information that has a rich set of features. The latter is developed in different ways. Whichever the case, cleaning the data is a must. This calls for fixing issues with the data points, filling missing values where it is possible and in some situations removing noisy elements.

Before the variables are used in a model, you must perform normalization on them. This is achieved using a linear transformation on making sure that the variable values rotate around a given range. Usually, normalization is enough for one to turn variables into features once they are cleaned.

Binning is another process which facilitates featurization. It involves building nominal variables which can further be broken down into different binary features applied in a data model.

Lastly, some reduction methods are important in building a feature set. This involves building a linear combination of features that display the same information in fewer dimensions.

Important Considerations

Besides the basic attributes of Data Science modeling, there are other important things that a Data Scientist must know to create something valuable. Things such as in-depth testing using specialized sampling, sensitivity analysis, and different aspects of the model performance to improve a given performance aspect belong to Data Science modeling.

The Future of Data Science and Predictive Modeling

There's no question on how predictive analytics is important. The new algorithm-based discipline has empowered us to deliver insights on the probability of a given outcome.

Use cases of Data Science and predictive modeling appear like trip-planning tools to help customers define locations, dates, hotel needs, and other factors which impact travel details. These products represent an evolution toward a user-friendly Data Science tool that can change a customer into a Data Scientist.

From Predictive to Prescriptive

Data Scientists are shifting toward a practical application of prescriptive instead of predictive modeling. While the latter applies historical data to predict the probability of future events, the former makes an assumption that an active human agent is capable of affecting outcomes.

Quick definitions

- **Descriptive analytics:** This represents the first stage of business analytics where you look at historical data and performance.

- **Prescriptive analytics:** This represents the third stage of business analytics where one determines the best course of action to take.

- **Predictive analytics:** This is the second stage of business analytics where you choose the best course of action.

Data Scientists can create a prescriptive uplift model to determine the chances of converting a lead with a given offer. For example, to determine whether sending a sign-on bonus can affect a prospective employee's chances of accepting a job.

This way, it becomes important for proactive planning. In addition, it creates a line difference between machine and human interactions. Older predictive models, for example, provide end users with insight into the likelihood of an event. It is then left to human agents to decide on what they can do with that information.

However, the prescriptive uplift model can determine the events of an outcome if the end users decide to follow a given course of action. Therefore, it helps determine if a marketing campaign can win over a given demographic or provide solutions for a political campaign to win votes.

The prospective applications of this type of proactive data are unmeasured. They are especially important when a person wants to predict results in retail, marketing, politics, and charitable donations.

Deep Learning: Machines Performing the Processing Patterns

The response to prescriptive modeling is a significant development as a result of the popularity of Machine Learning technologies. Modern Data Scientists are called to closely work with software engineers to develop new automated tools.

Most of these tools that they create use Machine Learning technology. The chances are that you might have heard of technological development. It is very popular in the Data Science field. But the thing that is most popular is Machine Learning because of how it relates to the Big Data and Data Science.

Machine Learning provides powerful applications of Big Data and statistical probability. It helps break down divisions that exist between data processing and data collection.

In this case, the machine continuously adjusts its behavior and responds depending on the environmental data. A good example of this is Amazon's recommendation tool – the more data that is fed into the tool by users via buying and browsing, the more precise the recommendation.

Tools such as these represent evidence of real-time interaction between devices and humans. While humans respond to results, machines customize their next offerings depending on the feedback. This is like a conversation compared to a chain of commands.

Deep Learning is a branch of Machine Learning. It models a structure and processes patterns of the human mind. Deep Learning computers are created using neural networks that have layers of nodes developed on top of one another. This kind of architecture creates connections with another nonlinear fashion.

Technologies in Deep Learning are important at emulating the type of visual processing carried out by the brain when it responds to signals from the eyes. For example, Google Translate app has Deep Learning to translate unembedded text from images into another language. A user that is traveling into a different country can take a picture of a box of cereal and upload it to Google Translate. Google can then identify text on the box and return a translation in the native language.

In the same way, there is another Google project called Google Sunroof which takes images from the Google Earth application and builds 3D models of rooftops using a solar installation. By using Deep Learning neural networks, the Sunroof tool can distinguish roof surfaces from cars or trees, even when obscuring factors exist such as tree coverage and shadow.

Deep Learning tools such as these permit Data Scientists to develop predictive models depending on the unstructured data like audio, video, and images instead of depending on structured information such as numbers and text.

Data Science Converging with AI

Both Deep Learning and Machine Learning are applications of Artificial Intelligence and the ever-changing use of AI technologies. These kinds of applications heavily affect the practice of Data Science. AI intelligence tools extend the data gathering process to data processing and go even a step further to synthesize data into solutions and designs.

For example, the Autodesk's Project Dreamcatcher uses AI to produce 3D product designs depending on criteria generated by designers such as functional objectives, manufacturing methods, and budget.

The distinction between this kind of project and other tools is that it doesn't only let users create designs. However, it provides different sets of data depending on solutions and allows designers to create prototypes that focus on customized problems.

Such tools expect a future where Data Science shifts from a strict analytical function and delivers insights and recommendations to product development and R & D applications.

Apart from AI tools performing human functions, they also do it most effectively. Machines like these can determine insights that only humans can feel. For instance, the Affectiva applies AI equipment to identify human emotions such as joy, anger, and surprise.

End of Human-Driven Data Science

The success of automated Machine Learning tools has led to the argument of whether there will be a time when human experts won't be necessary at all. The advanced nature of neural networks might very well automate the role of neural networks, and this could also automate the work of Data Scientists.

Chapter 14: Five Mining Techniques Data Scientists Require for Their Own Toolbox

One of the major strengths of Data Scientists is a strong background in Math and Statistics. Mathematics helps them create complex analytics. Besides this, they also use mathematics to create Machine Learning models and Artificial Intelligence. Similar to software engineering, Data Scientists must interact with the business side. This involves mastering the domain so that they can draw insights. Data Scientists need to analyze data to help a business, and this calls for some business acumen. Lastly, the results need to be assigned to the business in a way that anyone can understand. This calls for the ability to verbally and visually communicate advanced results and observations in a manner that a business can understand as well as work on it.

Therefore, it is important for any wannabe Data Scientists to have knowledge about Data Mining. Data Mining describes the process where raw data is structured in such a way where one can recognize patterns in the data via mathematical and computational algorithms.

Below are five mining techniques that every data scientist should know:

1. MapReduce

The modern Data Mining applications need to manage vast amounts of data rapidly. To deal with these applications, one must use a new software stack. Since programming systems can retrieve parallelism from a computing cluster, a software stack has a new file system called a distributed file system.

The system has a larger unit than the disk blocks found in the normal operating system. A distributed file system replicates data to enforce security against media failures.

In addition to such file systems, a higher-level programming system has also been created. This is referred to as MapReduce. It is a form of computing which has been implemented in different systems such as Hadoop and Google's implementation. You can adopt a MapReduce implementation to control large-scale computations such that it can deal with hardware faults. You only need to write three functions. That is **Map** and **Reduce**, and then you can allow the system to control parallel execution and task collaboration.

2. Distance Measures

The major problem with Data Mining is reviewing data for similar items. An example can be searching for a collection of web pages and discovering duplicate pages. Some of these pages could be plagiarism or pages that have almost identical content but different in content. Other examples can include customers who buy similar products or discover images with similar characteristics.

Distance measure basically refers to a technique that handles this problem. It searches for the nearest neighbors in a higher dimensional space. For every application, it is important to define the meaning of similarity. The most popular definition is the Jaccard Similarity. It refers to the ratio between intersection sets and union. It is the best similarity to reveal textual similarity found in documents and certain behaviors of customers.

For example, when looking for identical documents, there are different instances for this particular example. There might be very many small pieces of one document appearing out of order, more documents for comparisons, and documents that are so large to fit in the main memory. To handle these issues, there are three important steps to finding similar documents.

- *Shingling.* This involves converting documents into sets.

- *Min-Hashing.* It involves converting a large set into short signatures while maintaining similarity.

- *Locality Sensitive Hashing.* Concentrate on signature pairs that might be from similar documents.

The most powerful way that you can represent documents assets is to retrieve a set of short strings from the document.

- A k-Shingle refers to any k characters that can show up in a document.

- A min-hash functions on sets.

- Locality-Sensitive Hashing.

3. Link Analysis

Traditional search engines did not provide accurate search results because of spam vulnerability. However, Google managed to overcome this problem by using the following technique:

- PageRank. It uses simulation. If a user surfing a web page starts from a random page, PageRank attempts to congregate in case it had monitored specific outlines from the page that users are located. This whole process works iteratively meaning pages that have a higher number of users are ranked better than pages without users visiting.

- The content in a page was determined by the specific phrases used in the page and linked with external pages. Although it is easy for a spammer to modify a page that they are administrators, it is very difficult for them to do the same on an external page which they aren't administrators.

In other words, PageRank represents a function which allocates a real number to a web page. The intention is that a page with a higher page rank becomes more important than a page that does not have a page rank. There is no fixed algorithm defined to assign a page rank, but there are of different variety.

For powerfully connected Web Graphs, PageRank applies the principle of transition matrix. This principle is useful for calculating the rank of a page.

To calculate the behavior of a page rank, it simulates the actions of random users on a page.

There are different enhancements that one can make to PageRank. The first one is called Topic-Sensitive PageRank. This type of improvement can weigh certain pages more heavily as a result of their topic. If you are aware of the query in a particular page, then it is possible to be biased on the rank of the page.

4. Data Streaming

In most of the Data Mining situations, you can't know the whole data set in advance. There are times when data arrives in the form of a stream, and then gets processed immediately before it disappears forever.

Furthermore, the speed at which data arrives very fast, and that makes it hard to store in the active storage. In short, the data is infinite and non-stationary. Stream management, therefore, becomes very important.

In the data stream management system, there is no limit to the number of streams that can fit into a system. Each data stream produces elements at its own time. The elements should then have the same data rates and time in a particular stream.

Streams can be archived into a store, but this will make it impossible to reply to queries from the archival store. This can later be analyzed under special cases by using a specific retrieval method.

Furthermore, there is a working store where summaries are placed so that one can use to reply to queries. The active store can either be a disk or main memory. It all depends on the speed at which one wants to process the queries. Whichever way, it does not have the right capacity to store data from other streams.

Data streaming has different problems as highlighted below:

- **Sampling Data in a Stream**

To create a sample of the stream that is used in a class of queries, you must select a set of attributes to be used in a stream. By hashing the key of an incoming stream element, the hash value can be the best to help determine whether all or none of the elements in the key belong to the sample.

- **Filtering Streams**

To accept tuples that fit a specific criterion, accepted tuples should go through a separate process of the stream while the rest of the tuples are eliminated. Bloom filtering is a wonderful technique that one can use to filter streams to allow elements in a given set to pass through while foreign elements are deleted.

Members in the selected set are hashed into buckets to form bits. The bits are then set to 1. If you would like to test an element of a stream, you must hash the element into a set of bits using the hash function.

- **Count Specific Elements in a Stream**

Consider stream elements chosen from a universal set. If you wanted to know the number of unique elements that exist in a stream, you might have to count from the start of the stream. Flajolet-Martin is a method which often hashes elements to integers, described as binary numbers. By using a lot of the hash functions and integrating these estimates, you finally get a reliable estimate.

5. Frequent Item – Set Analysis

The market-basket model features many relationships. On one side, there are items, and on the opposite side, there are baskets. Every basket contains a set of items. The hypothesis created here is that the number of items in the basket is always smaller than the total number of items. This means that if you count the items in the basket, it should be high and large to fit in memory. Here, data is similar to a file that has a series of baskets. In reference to the distributed file system, baskets represent the original file. Each basket is of type "set of items".

As a result, a popular family technique to characterize data depending on the market-basket model is to discover frequent item-sets. These are sets of items that reveal the most baskets.

Market basket analysis was previously applied in supermarket and chain stores. These stores track down the contents of each market basket that a customer brings to the checkout. Items represent products sold by the store while baskets are a set of items found in a single basket.

That said, this same model can be applied in many different data types such as:

- **Similar concepts.** Let items represent words and baskets documents. Therefore, a document or basket has words or items available in the document. If you were to search for words that are repeated in a document, sets would contain the most words.

- **Plagiarism.** You can let the items represent documents and baskets to be sentenced.

Properties of Frequent-Item Sets to Know

- **Association rules**. These refer to implications in case a basket has a specific set of items.

- **Monotonicity**. One of the most important properties of item-sets is that if a set is frequent, then all its subsets are frequent.

Chapter 15: The Concept of Decision Trees in Data Science

Decision trees are a powerful and simple type of multiple variable analyses. This offers a unique functionality to complement for:

- Data variety mining techniques and tools
- Traditional methods of analysis
- Recently invented multidimensional methods of analysis and reporting in the field of intelligence.

Decision trees are generated by algorithms which have different forms of splitting data into segments. These segments combine to become an inverted decision tree that has a root node as the origin at the top of the tree. The purpose of the analysis is identified in the root node. This can be a simple, one-dimensional display in the decision tree interface. The main field of data analysis is shown alongside the distribution of values found in the field. A simple decision tree is shown below. This particular type of tree represents a continuous and categorical form of objective analysis.

A decision tree is guided by the decision rule where it must form branches below the root node. This originated from a method which identifies the relationship between object analysis and target field and many other fields which act as input to build branches. The values contained in the input are referred to as response or a dependent variable.

Once the relationship is developed, then it becomes easy to build a decision tree which describes the relationship that exists between inputs and targets. Rules can then be selected and used to demonstrate the decision tree that offers a way in which you can visually describe and examine the tree-like network relationship.

Decision trees have the potential to predict new values or hidden observations that have values for specific inputs but may be without values for specific targets.

The decision tree rule allocates every derived observation from the data set to a segment depending on the value of one of the columns in the data. Columns that are taken to build rules are referred to as inputs. Still, there are splitting rules in decision trees. These rules are applied one after the other to help build a nest of branches that generate the general shape of a decision tree. The hierarchy of branches is called a decision tree, and every segment in the tree is called a node. If a node has all its children, it forms an extra segment or branch of the node. Nodes at the bottom of the decision tree are called leaves.

For every leaf, the decision tree has a special path for data to get into the class defined as the leaf. All nodes in the decision tree share a rule referred to as a mutually exclusive assignment rule. Therefore, records and observations from the parent data set can only exist in a single node alone. Once the decision trees are defined, it is then easy to use the rules to generate other node values depending on the unseen data. In predictive modeling, a decision tree will generate a predicted value.

The idea of a decision tree came to life more than 50 years ago; the earliest decision tree was used in the study of television broadcasting in 1956 by Belson. From that time, many different types of decision trees were developed that aim to offer new capabilities in the field of Data Mining and Machine Learning. For instance, one form of the decision tree involved the development of random forests.

A random forest consisted of multi-tree committees which apply a randomly drawn sample of data and inputs. In addition, it has a rewarding technique to build multiple trees which, when integrated, generate a strong prediction about the structure of the decision tree.

Apart from data modeling, you can use a decision tree to explore and categorize data for dimensional cubes that exist in business analytics and Business Intelligence.

Applying the Decision Tree with More Modeling Techniques

Decision trees work best with other modeling techniques like regression. These techniques are important at selecting inputs or generating dummy variables to represent the effects of interaction in equations dealing with regression.

The main point in stratified regression is to identify and understand that relationship in data is not easily fitted for linear regression equation.

Another reason why decision trees are used in Data Science is that they collapse a group of categorical values into specific ranges aligned with the values of a given target variable. This is also called optimal value collapsing. A normal method to collapse categorical values together is to combine categories into one. Since decision trees support a combination of categories with similar values concerning the level of certain target values, there is a very minimum information loss in collapsing categories together. This results in an improved prediction and classification results.

Why Are Decision Trees Very Important?

Decision trees are a type of multiple variable analyses. All types of multiple variable analyses allow us to explain, describe, and classify the target. An example of a multiple variable that includes analysis is the probability of sale or chance to respond to a marketing campaign due to the effects of multiple input variables, dimensions, and factors. The multiple variable analysis abilities of decision trees allow an individual to explore other relationships and discover as well as explain things in the context of multiple influences.

In fact, multiple variable analyses are essential in current modern problem-solving – since every critical outcome that determines success depends on multiple factors. Additionally, it is now getting clear that even if it is easy to build a single-cause, this approach may result in a costly and misleading outcome.

According to different studies done in psychology, it has been discovered that the ability to properly master and manipulate different chunks of knowledge is limited by both the physical and cognitive limitations in processing. This adds up on the utilization of dimensional presentation techniques and manipulation that are capable of reflecting and preserving a high-dimensional relationship in a more comprehensive way.

There are many multiple variable techniques present. The attractive side of decision trees depends on their ease of use, robustness, and relative power with different data and level of measurements. Decision trees are constructed and presented in an incremental style. Therefore, the joined set of multiple influences is a group of one-cause, one-effect relationships demonstrated in the recursive type of decision tree.

This implies that a decision tree handles human short memory issues in an effective way and in a manner that is easy to understand than complex, multiple variable techniques. Decision trees transform raw data into a detailed knowledge and awareness of business, scientific, and engineering issues. This allows one to deploy knowledge in a simple but yet powerful human readable form.

Decision trees try to discover a strong relationship between input values and target values in a set of observations that build a data set. In case a set of input values is selected as having a specific association with a target value, all the target values are classified into a bin that forms a branch on the decision tree.

This specific kind of grouping is highlighted by the observed relationship between bin values and the target. For instance, if the average target value is very different in the three bins created by the input, then binning will select every input and determine how the input values are linked to the target.

A robust input-target relationship develops when knowledge about the value of input enhances the ability to predict the value of the target. A strong relationship will allow you to understand the nature of the target. It is therefore okay for this type of relationship to be used to predict the values of the targets.

Conclusion

In the final chapter, this book examined the important concepts that the best Data Scientists know and apply in carrying out Data Science tasks. Machine Learning, defined as the practice of using algorithms to analyze data and learning from it, is the key for a Data Scientist to help forecast future trends.

The practice of Data Science can best be explained as a combination of statistical analysis, Big Data, and Data Mining. Businesses, companies, and large organizations have problems that Data Scientists need to solve. Usually, most of these problems may not be part of the standard Data Mining tasks. Therefore, Data Scientists may need to divide the problem into smaller chunks that are solvable often beginning with existing tools. For some tasks, you may well not know how to solve it. That is where Data Mining comes into play. By carefully applying Data Mining techniques learned in this book, you can easily overcome some of the challenges that you face.

Don't forget that to become the best Data Scientist you need to ensure that you have a strong analytical mind to help you create effective business solutions. Although you may not have all the skills and knowledge that the best Data Scientists have, everything has its starting point. If you can ensure that you spend most of your time learning and mastering what the best Data Scientists know, then you can be sure to achieve a lot in your journey of data analysis.

Part 2: Data Science for Business

Predictive Modeling, Data Mining, Data Analytics, Data Warehousing, Data Visualization, Regression Analysis, Database Querying, and Machine Learning for Beginners

Introduction

The following chapters will discuss everything that you need to know to get started as a beginner in data science.

Data science is a new industry that is gaining popularity because of the valuable resources and information that it provides to companies and businesses. They can use the information in the findings of data scientists to help make important decisions that will reduce risks, make profits, avoid issues in the future, and serve customers better.

This guidebook will go through the basics of data science. It will discuss what data science is, how to get started with it, and some of the algorithms that you can learn to use to get the information. It will also talk about data mining text and the special challenges this presents to data scientists, and even how to present the information so that it makes sense to those who would use it to make major business decisions.

When you are ready to get started with data science, read this book and see how you can do it too!

Chapter 1: What is Data Science?

Many businesses already know that there is extraordinary potential for the data that they hold onto. They already have this data from their customers and other sources; they just need to be able to harness it and learn how to use it properly. Many of these companies do not know how to harness this material, and they may not have the soft skill or the technical requirements to do data science, which is why this has become a field of work in high demand. For those who already know how to do this kind of thing, you can really become a valuable asset for a business. However, let's take a look at some of the basics of data science first to determine how to get started with this and what it all means.

What is data science?

Data science is a field that helps the user understand events or gain useful information simply by going through data and analyzing it. The results of the analysis are then going to be used to create a decision. This decision is often made by a company to help them better serve their customers, make a newer and better product, and more. These kinds of decisions are also known as data-driven decisions, and they are used to improve decision-making skills, mainly in business, which is the end goal of data science.

At first glance, it is easy to think that data science is the same as statistics. However, when we talk about statistics, we are just talking about one type of data science. Data science will work with a variety of fields, such as computer science, information science, mathematics, and statistics, to generate information from a set of data that can aid the user to make important decisions.

Data-driven decision making

The main idea of data science is to work on data-driven decision making. Data-driven decision making is the discipline of creating decisions that have the backing of analyzed data that has been collected from some relevant sources. Without this kind of data, it is easy to base your decisions on experience, intuition, or on what others tell you are the right decisions. However, all of these can be wrong, even though there is a chance that they would be like.

With data-driven decision making, it is easier to make smart decisions and then back it up with proof. Sometimes it can be combined with knowledge, intuition, and experience to come up with the best decisions. For example, someone who has worked in the industry for a long time would be able to use the information they get from data science along with their intuition and experience to make the best decisions.

Of course, there are not really set rules when it comes to the process of data-driven decision making. Many organizations use it to a varying degree based on what they are looking for. Some companies choose to fully rely on this kind of technology, and they will automate it in certain areas of decision making in their organization. One example of this is how Amazon can recommend products based on the purchases that the user has put in their shopping cart.

Other companies would use people to design a personal data collection, using technology to collect this data and then analyze it, and then will use all that information to make decisions based on them. Google does this to determine if managers are making a difference in how well their team is performing.

Applications of data science

You will find that there are many applications when it comes to using data science for business organizations, public agencies, and nonprofit organizations. Government financial agencies and even some banking corporations use data science to determine a lot of things, such as protecting their bank holders from identity theft and bank fraud and to figure out who may be a possible money launderer. Websites and other online stores will use some automated approaches to create decisions driven by data to customize advertisements to their target customers.

This is not all of course. Social media websites and their applications have started to use facial recognition algorithms to help them make automated tagging features. This is seen in applications like Facebook. Their algorithm can sometimes figure out who is in a picture using these features. On-demand music and video streaming services base their recommendations to the user based on the browsing history of the user.

These are just a few of the examples of the applications of this type of science. Basically, any organization that would like to collect data and then use it to figure out major decisions in the future will find that data science can work for them. Some companies will do the work on their own and add in some of their knowledge and experience about the industry to help them make decisions. Moreover, some may hire out and get a professional data scientist to help them look over the information to provide a report back. Either way, the business is planning on going through the information to figure out how to make good decisions for their company in the near or far away future with the information they get out of the data.

Regardless of the organization or industry, data science can really be used to help improve the efficiency of the whole organization and to improve customer or user experience. This can help managers, and the owners of the company, learn how to make smarter decisions to help them make more money.

How is data science done?

Since the word "science" is used inside of the name, data science is sometimes seen as a scientific approach to extracting knowledge or other insight from the data. Just like you did with the scientific approach, data science will begin with the use of observation.

In this case, the act of observation will include an analysis of data. This can be done through either an automated or manual means, to bring about patterns from that information. There is also the chance to formulate a hypothesis by verifying the observed patterns as valid, rather than just getting a coincidence of data. Lastly, you will also need to do some testing to verify the created model that you are given.

In addition to being a type of science, data science can be seen as a field of study that is still in its infancy. Because it is still so new, there are some different opinions and positions as to the process of how it should be done. In this book, we will look at three approaches to help you gain a level of understanding and appreciation.

The benefits and negatives of data science

The first question that a business will have before they get started with data science for their needs is the benefits and the negatives of data science. First, we are going to take a look at some of the benefits to see how it can help the business.

The first benefit is that it can help the business to make some important decisions. In the past, the business had to rely on their experience and knowledge about the market and their industry to figure out whether they were making smart choices. Those who had been in the industry for a long time could be good at this, but they may still miss out on important information that could help them out. Those who are new to the industry could easily make a lot of mistakes.

The data science field helps managers and decision-makers look at information from different sources to help them make better decisions. They may be able to figure out which products to develop, how to provide better customer service, and even if there are new demographics to put their marketing efforts towards.

With the right data science techniques, the information can be combed through in no time at all. This information is often so big that it would take years or more for a person to go through and by then, the information would be out of date. The data science field would be able to help you get through this information in no time so that you can actually use it in real time to help make your business stronger.

However, it is important to realize that you need to look through the data and not always just take it at face value. There is often a lot of great information that is collected with data science, but if you are not careful, you may get the wrong information out of it. You need to take an objective look at the information to see if it makes sense. And then add in what you already know about the industry and the market to see if you can combine those to really propel your business forward.

Blitzstein and Pfister

The first step in this data science process is to ask a question that is interesting. During this stage, you will use the information that you know, as well as your curiosity about a subject, your experiences, and any expertise that you have to formulate questions. This can help you direct the way that you analyze the information that you are presented. Some of the questions that you may want to try out during this stage include:

- What is the goal?
- What would you like to do if you had access to all of the data?
- What would you like to estimate or predict?

After you formulate your question, it is time to move on to the second step. This step is when you will get the data. There are several computer processes you can use for this including querying databases, data cleaning, and web scraping. You may have a few more questions that you can ask during this stage to help move it along such as:

- How were the data sampled and will that affect the results that you get?
- Which pieces of data are the most relevant?
- Are there any issues of privacy to consider?

From here, you can move on to the next step which is exploring the data. You will want to start with familiarizing yourself with it, developing different hypotheses regarding the data, and then determining possible patterns as well as anomalies that may show up in the data that you will collect. Some of the questions that you may get for this stage include:

1. How can this data be plotted
2. Are there any patterns present?
3. Are there any anomalies in the data that you have?

Under this method, you would move onto the fourth step. This step is to model the data that you have. You could use a few different options including big data technologies, data validation, machine learning and regression analysis to make this happen.

And then you will move on to the last step. This is where you will communicate with the data through an easily understood manner of presentation either through writing, visualizing, and speaking. Valuable questions to effectively ask to make sure that you can do this include:

- What did we learn?

- Do the results that we are getting make sense?
- Can we tell a story from the results that we get?

Provost and Fawcett

With this model, the data science will be presented as an area that is separate from the big data technologies, data procession, and data engineering. It will differentiate itself because it will use those areas to help aid in formulating a decision driven by data that is made across the firm, which is considered by this model as the end goal of data science. It won't consider the other things because these could be used only to improve various processes in the organization, but they are not really there to help aid in the decision-making process.

O'Neill and Schutt

Another model that you can use is the O'Neil and Schutt model. With this one, data is collected from various sources in the environment. This could include a platform that the users of interest can interact with, a website, or another type of database. The data that is collected from this source is processed to produce a clean data set, and then it will usually be presented in a data table. This data set will be used for a few things such as statistical modeling and data analysis.

The result of this analysis is then going to produce either a new data set or a new type of data that you would then be able to process for another data set. Both of these are used to complete further statistical modeling. The result here is that they could be a data product that will be sent back to the environment or it is a report that could be used to make decisions in the company.

Exploratory data analysis

This approach analyzes data sets to summarize them out into their main characteristics. This may be presented as a visual aid or in some other manner. For the most part, this analysis is used to visualize what the data can present beyond hypothesis testing and formal modeling tasks. In some cases, the results that you get could be used to help with statistical models. We will spend more time covering these in a later chapter.

Statistical modeling

Another thing that we need to discuss concerning data science is statistical modeling. This is a model that will approximate a real-world phenomenon, and then it can sometimes predict from that approximation using some simple mathematical equations. Depending on where you decide to apply this kind of modeling, the equation could be shown as a simple linear regression, or it could be as complicated as a multivariate factor analysis.

The equation that is there to explain the phenomenon, depending on the size of the data that you are looking to model, could be obtained through either automated or manual means depending on the what you would use the results for. When it comes to the case of data science, the amount of data that the analysts would use is often going to require them to go with software that can automate the process. There is just too much data present to try and go through it all manually, and it would take too long, and human error would cause something to be missed.

The difference between exploring and explaining

When it comes to data science, there are two schools of thoughts that are taking the lead. The first one is a group of those who believe that the use of data science should be there to satisfy the curiosity of the user. They believe that going through the data to find the different phenomena and patterns that are there should be enough for the data scientists and they shouldn't need to do anything else with it.

There is also the second school of thought which believes that this information should be used. It may not be enough just to see the information. This group believes that the patterns and the phenomena that are found in the data should be used by companies and organizations to create decisions. Whether the company decides to do this manually or automatically doesn't matter.

If you are using data science for business, it is likely that you are going to fall in with the second group of thinkers. You will want to use the information and patterns that you collect from your analysis of the data to make decisions for the business. These decisions could be about how to serve your customers better, what products to try out, and what important decisions to make in the future. No matter what, you are using the information to help you make important business decisions.

Chapter 2: How Big Data Works in Data Science

To get started with data science, you must first understand where the information that you will be using comes from. Data science is not possible without any data present – or else you wouldn't have anything to analyze in the process. Moreover, with the infrastructure that is provided by different technologies – that process a lot of information efficiently – many companies are starting to take advantage of sources like the internet to collect information. This is where Big Data will come in.

Let's take a closer look at Big Data so we can learn how it works in data science.

The definition of Big Data

To keep it simple, Big Data are data sets that are too complex or too large to be captured and managed or processed in a bearable time by using tools that are common. Using the relational database management system would not work because there is too much information to process so it would take too long.

Because there was not much software to help keep up with this, and companies still wanted to be able to go through all that information to help make decisions, new database platforms were created. These include such options as Hadoop and NoSQL.

When talking about Big Data, there are five unique data characteristics. The three main ones include:

- *Volume*: This is the amount of data that is produced or received by the company in a day. This would amount to terabytes. Because of this, the volume of the Big Data will be so large that it must be stored on several different servers. This can also present a big challenge because it would take an unreasonable amount of time to analyze the data if it is done manually.
- *Velocity*: The Big Data has to be available as close to real-time as possible. The faster that the right people can get to the data, the better advantage they will have to make good decisions for their business. The information that you collected even an hour ago could end up losing its relevance by the time you can do anything with it.
- *Variety*: Data needs to come from many different formats or sources. You may be able to get Big Data from smartphone GPS data, in-house devices, forums, social network trends, and even comments on social networks. The variety that you get your data from will provide you with a better data set.

Types of data

There are three main types of data: structured, unstructured, and semi-structured.

Structured data has a predetermined format and length. The pieces of information that come with structured data are ones that can be sorted, grouped, and organized quickly. A good example of this is what you can find when looking at databases like Access and SQL.

Unstructured data is the kind that does not have a predetermined format. It is hard for an individual to be efficient when going through the information. They would need software and algorithms to go through the information efficiently. Some examples of this would include documents, emails, social media posts, videos, and photos.

Semi-structured data is any data that will not fit into relational databases or data tables, but it still contains some attributes and tags. This type is often called *self-describing data*. This means that the structure will have embedded itself in the data. Examples of this would be JavaScript Object Notation and Extensible Markup Language, which are different data-driven mobile applications.

The architecture of Big Data

You will find that when working with Big Data, it will come in five layers. Let's look at each layer and see what they will mean for your data:

Layer 0

Big Data requires a physical infrastructure that is redundant to handle the enormous requirements to compute it. This infrastructure will be linked by a network to enable the sharing of resources between the computers that hold the information, and it is there to create backups of the information in case there is a computer failure along the way. The performance, availability, scalability, flexibility, and the cost of this infrastructure are all important, and you need to take them into account before starting.

Layer 1

There needs to be the right amount of security to make sure that the data inside will stay safe. It is often necessary to use high-grade encryption so that no one can mess with the integrity of the data. Security measures need to also be in place so that you can detect threats to the data, such as a data leak, and data loss should also be taken into account. Access to the data and all the applications surrounding it need to be minimized so that there are fewer risks from human error.

Layer 2

The infrastructure needs to employ the storage of all types of data, including the three types that were discussed earlier. There needs to also be some atomicity, consistency, isolation, and the durability of the infrastructure's, or database's, behavior.

Layer 3

It is important for the infrastructure to be organized and compiled using technologies that are from a distributed filed system. It also needs things like serialization and coordination services, ETL tools, and workflow services.

Layer 4

Finally, the infrastructure should consolidate data gathered from relational and other databases for ease of access for later analysis.

The benefits of using Big Data

With all the work that comes with Big Data, you may wonder why someone would want to work with it rather than trying to work with something else? There are actually many great benefits that come with Big Data. To start, Big Data can provide a company or business with valuable data that they can use for risk analysis. Supply managers create demand forecasts and supply planning in anticipation, and mitigate any variance to resource availability.

Big Data is also a good way to help manufacturing businesses improve operational efficiency. When sensors are added for operations analytics at the assembly line, this means that the managers of production can collect data and then create a model that they can use to improve the efficiency of the company – if the information is used properly.

Big Data further helps a business explore better revenue opportunities and whether they are good ideas or not. With a business that is trying to grow, this can be a big deal. They will be able to improve how efficiently they can do research and development so that they will pick out the right products that help them to get the best results with their customers.

Moreover, Big Data helps businesses when they are looking to improve their customer service. When the business has a way to collect consumer feedback, they can create a new database on customer profile and the feedback that they get. They can also use this to adjust their operations and the services that they provide to their customers according to the information that they receive.

Risks of using Big Data

While there are a lot of great benefits that come from using Big Data, there are also some risks. Data analysts and engineers who don't conduct the proper design and analysis create inadequate data, with a wrong analysis. This ends up with the wrong data that would be used for decisions in the business. If the information is read the wrong way, it could create a big loss of resources for the business and could result in many other problems.

There is also the risk of Big Data being stolen for nefarious and fraudulent purposes. If this does happen on a large scale for a business, it means that the customers will stop trusting the company and money will be lost as well. This can be hard to regain in the future.

In addition, maintaining the infrastructure for using Big Data could be expensive. Having this kind of data in the company, and trying to use it to improve the operations of the business or increase the revenue, can be two different things. Proper planning and goal setting for this kind of data are important to consider before investing it in the company.

The context of data

It is important that while you can get a lot of information out of Big Data, having access to it is not necessarily enough to gain a competitive advantage through data science. Context is just as important, as it gives meaning to what the whole data is about. You need to know what that data means and be able to interpret it properly – or else you are just going to have a bunch of data that is not going to get you ahead of the competition.

Data with the right context can formulate business problems that seek the reasons as to why an event happened compared to only seeking what happened. With the right context, it is easier for the business to understand why things happened. And with the right understanding, a business is better equipped to take advantage of the opportunities that are there for a similar event. It can also take the right actions to correct things if it looks like there may be something harmful to their sales or operations.

Without the context in place for the Big Data, it is hard to figure out what the data means. However, when the company knows what they are looking for, use the context of the industry, and know what is going on with the economy, and the feedback that they are getting from their customers, they find that it is much easier to understand the Big Data that they receive. Furthermore, they can use that information to help them progress into the future.

Chapter 3: Explorative Data Analysis

With the help of all the available technologies that are out there to help automate data analysis, it is easier to take for granted why there may be a benefit of having the human mind and eye look over the data that you have. A study or research and the results that you get is only as good as the quality of the data used in it.

This means that even with technology, a data scientist needs to investigate the quality of the data that is used. They should not just look at the information that they are presented with and take it at face value. They need to look and see if it is high-quality or if something seems wrong with the process. This is where explorative data analysis can be beneficial.

It is not always a good idea to rely on the information that the other methods are presenting. Sometimes they are great, but it is always best to go through and make sure that the information makes sense. Those who just take the information that they receive, and then run with it to make their decisions, may find it works at some points, but it is not going to be the best bet. In fact, it will often lead to making poor decisions for a business and running it into the ground.

It is much better to take a look at the data. You can use some of the other methods out there that have the technology to help; however, then you need to go through and check the information and make sure that it makes sense before you run with the information.

What is this explorative data analysis?

Explorative data analysis, or EDA, is a method of analyzing data sets so that you can summarize them out into their main characteristics. You can use a statistical model to do this, but EDA is there to see what a data set can tell you beyond formal modeling or hypothesis testing. However, it is more concerned with observational data than data from formally design testing. It is not confined to a set of techniques, but a philosophy about how the data analysis should be done.

When you are ready to use EDO, you need to remember that the techniques are used with these goals in mind:

- To help detect mistakes in the data
- To check any assumptions presented with the data

- To help with a preliminary selection of appropriate models
- To assess the relationships and the direction of the different variables.

Make sure that you are not mistaking the EDA with the initial data analysis, which will focus on checking assumptions that are necessary for model fitting and hypothesis testing. It can even handle missing values and adjust the variables – if you need to ensure that you get the right information from the data.

Types of EDA

There are a few different types of EDA that you can work on. The one that you will want to choose will depend on the information that you want to use and what you want to do with the data that you have. Some of the types of EDA include:

Univariate non-graphical EDA

This is the first step to analyzing the data. With this type, there will be just one variable or characteristic that is being observed, and that is used to help represent the sample. Usually, the objective of univariate non-graphical EDA is to create a better appreciation of the sample distribution and to help carefully conclude the compatible population distribution and sample distribution. Since this is a non-graphical method, the data used for it will be objective and qualitative.

Univariate graphical EDA

This focuses on a single variable of a sample distribution. However, when working with univariate graphical EDA, it will deal more with quantitative data rather than qualitative data. Some of the techniques include quantile-normal plots, boxplots, stem and leaf plots, and histograms.

Multivariate non-graphical EDA

This illustrates the relationship between at least two variables through cross-tabulation or statistics, like covariance and correlation.

Multivariate graphical EDA

This shows some of the relationships between variables; however, like the univariate graphical EDA, the data used is more quantitative. The technique that is used commonly for this is a grouped bar plat.

The type of EDA that you can use depends on the type of information that you are looking at, how much information you are going to work with, and what you would like to do with the information when you are all done. Each of these can work really well as long as you have an idea of what you are looking for out of the data. You can even experiment with the different ones to figure out what will work the best for your needs and what gives the best information.

Chapter 4: Working with Data Mining

The data that is stored in your databases and other infrastructures has a lot of potentials. However, taking the time to comb through all the data would end up being impractical if people had to go through all of it slowly. This is where the process of data mining comes in. It is a reliable and automated technology that is designed to seek out patterns that may be of interest to the business.

Exploring data could then be the next step after the owner or manager of the business ponder a problem that they think data science could solve – or it could help to provide an observation for a data scientist to look into that could provide valuable insight into improving the business. Data mining can make it easier to help get this done.

Let's take a look at how to get started with this process.

What is data mining?

Data mining is a process that is automated and aimed at data exploration. It finds patterns out of a large set of data using well-defined subtasks (which is discussed later). Data mining makes sense of all the large data regarding the absence or presence of the relationships between the variables. It can also look at the explanation of past actions and a prediction to future actions.

The inability to attain a solution to a problem when data mining is not considered is a failure in itself. Data mining is an exploration of data that could create a basis or a prediction for future data sets.

The tasks of data mining

As mentioned above, data mining has to rely on subtasks to find the patterns that may be present inside a large amount of data. Some of the tasks include the following:

Classification

This is the attempt to forecast which class each individual of a population in a large amount of data belongs to. This can help to separate out the information, so it is easier to understand and find the information needed. A good example of this in a business would be "In the existing customers of the company, which ones are most likely to respond to a given offer." This will have two categories: those who would respond and those who would not respond. It is possible to have many different categories based on what is trying to be figured out from the information.

Regression

This task attempts to estimate the numerical value of a variable for each part of the data set. The possible variables could include things such as the rate of usage for the service based on the historical usage of each person in the data set.

Similarity matching

As the name implies, this task tries to identify individuals in the population that have similar variables to those individuals that are selected out of the population. A good example of this is to find individuals that will match the variables for the customers who are seen as the best option for the company.

The similarity underlies many data science methods and solutions to a problem of the business. If two things, such as a product company, and people, are similar in some ways, they are going to often come with different characteristics as well. Data mining procedures can be based on grouping things by similarity or by allowing the search for the similarity needed.

This was seen with some of the previous chapters – where modeling procedures create boundaries to group instances together when they come with similar values for the target variables. Later in this chapter, we are going to take a look at the similarity in more detail and show how it will be applied to a variety of tasks.

Clustering

This task attempts to group individuals of a data set based on the similarities that they have, without putting in any parameters. It is a time to explore, to find out the presence of groups in a set of data, and if there are groups, one can use the variables that create the said groups.

In some of the applications that you work with, you may want to look through to find groups of objects. For example, you could use it to find groups of customers, but not driven by some pre-specified target characteristic. You can use it to find out if your customers form some natural groups or segments among themselves? This could be useful in giving a business a view of the bigger picture, and then you can use this to market properly. It can also help decision-makers to ask some important questions like, *Do we really understand the people who shop with us?*

You can also use it to figure out what the customer needs. Could the business use it to develop some better marketing campaigns, better sales methods, better products, or better customer service by understanding the natural subgroups? This is a concept that will make a big difference to businesses in how they work with their customers. The basic idea with clustering is that you want to find groups of objects – whether they are customers, consumers, or something else – where the objects within groups are similar, but the objects that are found in different groups are not really similar.

You can also find hierarchical clusterings. These are often going to be formed by starting with each node that is part of its own cluster. Then the clusters are merged until there is only one main cluster left. These clusters are merged on a variety of factors, including their similarity or even the distance function that is chosen.

For hierarchical clustering, you need to have some distance function between clusters, considering individual instances to be the smallest clusters. This is often called the *linkage function*. For example, the linkage function could be the Euclidean distance between the closest points in each of the clusters, which could then apply to any two clusters.

Co-occurrence Grouping

This task attempts to find connections between entities that occurred in the same transactions. A good example is the recommendation feature of online shopping websites like Amazon. These recommendation features are going to present products that people have already purchased that are similar to what others have gotten.

Profiling

This attempts to set behavioral norms to an individual, a group, or a population's actions. It can also look at buying behavior, transaction locations, and service usage. This is often going to be used to detect anomalies in the behavior of a consumer and can be used when you want to look and see if there is an issue with fraud.

The two methods of data mining

Data mining through a set of data can be done in two ways: supervised and unsupervised.

When data mining is done in an unsupervised manner, the patterns and the structures will be sought in data that is unlabeled. This is usually used to create the basis for further data mining tasks, which are then going to be done supervised. The result of this is known as labeled data.

You can also use supervised data mining. These are done by going through your set of data with the labeled data as an aid. This labeled data will be used to identify individuals in the set of data. Identification could be based on any variable, such as a group, correlation, or causality. This labeled data could come from the data set that supervised data mining is being done or on a new data set.

Chapter 5: Data Mining Text

Text is another form of data, and like any other form of data that you want to work with, it can be transformed so that it is easier to analyze. Unfortunately, text works differently because it is an unstructured form of data and this can make it difficult when you want it analyzed by different types of technologies. However, when it comes to text, there is a lot of potential information, so it is hard to pass up on it.

The database of the company alone could hold a lot of information in the form of text. This could come in consumer complaint logs, medical records, product inquiries, and customer records. If this is done the right way, the data that is taken from text could help the business gain an insight into how their customers behave and into the preferences of their customers. Knowing this information would allow the business to create better services, products, and customer service.

A lot of the information that you are going to want from the Internet will come in the form of text. You will find this text on social media, blog posts, review articles, and personal web pages. Being able to get the information out of the text from these sources will make a big difference in how much data you can use.

The reason that text is so difficult to work with is due to the fact it is an unstructured data source that you would normally have in table links, fixed meaning, fields, and tables. It is meant to be understood by a human, but computers do not easily understand it. In addition to lots of different lengths of words, text fields, and even word orders, it is possible that people will write using the wrong spelling and grammar and also with random punctuations and abbreviations.

Because of all these variables, it becomes really hard to data mine the text that you want to use. The good news is that it is possible to take the text that you have and convert it to text.

How to convert your text into usable data

A body of text first needs to be changed into a set of data before you can feed it through an algorithm of data mining. This is generally done through the same technology that various search engines are going to use, such as Bing and Google. There are a few different options that you can use:

Bag of words

This approach converts text into a structured form. This is usually going to be in the feature-vector form. This treats each document as a simple collection of individual words. It won't look at it all as a whole but at each little part. It will also ignore punctuation, sentence structure, word order, and even grammar. Each individual word inside the document will be treated like a potential keyword that has some importance.

Many businesses like to use this method because it is easy and inexpensive to generate and it will work well for most of the tasks that they want to do with data mining.

Term frequency

With this approach, the system will look at how many times a word shows up in a particular document and then will use this to determine how important the term is. The more frequently it appears in the document, the more valuable and important that term is.

Every word in the document will first need to be converted so that it is in lowercase format. This will help because it would count words that are in different cases to be counted as the same thing. Also, words that are stemmed or have suffixes will be removed, so that the system can count the word, no matter what the original form is. And the stop words, or words that are really common, such as 'the', 'and', 'of' and 'on', will be removed, so they don't mess with the results of this test.

Inverse document frequency

This approach is used when measuring the frequency of a term in a collection of documents. It is not just responsible for measuring how often a term or a word appears though. It will impose an upper and a lower limit for the term to be considered as important. It is doing this to make sure that a specific term is not too rare or not too common to be included in the results.

Without this option, the data mining system would consider the distribution of words throughout the whole set of documents. This is because a term that may appear in fewer documents can sometimes be more significant in the documents that do contain it.

Here is a formula to use when looking for inverse document frequency:

IDF(t) = 1 + log(Total number of documents / number of documents containing t)

With this, the (t) will be for whatever term is being looked up.

TFIDF

Term frequency-inverse document frequency, or TFIDF, is a combination of the two approaches already discussed. It evaluates how important a term or a word is to the document inside a series of documents. The importance of this term will increase the more that it shows up in a document, but this can be offset by the frequency of said term when you look at all the documents. This approach is the one that search engines use when they want to score and rank to figure out if a web page or a document is relevant to a given search query. The formula for TFIDF is:

TFIDF(t, d) = TF(t, d) X IDF(t)

N-gram sequences

This approach counts the sequences of adjacent words as terms. An example of this is a sentence like, *The quick brown fox jumps.* When looking for this in a document, it will be considered as one whole term and tokens would be created, so it looks like quick_brown, brown_fox, and fox_jumps. This approach would be useful when the phrases are significant in a document but the words making up the phrases are not that important.

Named entity extraction

With the named entity extraction approach, the significant phrases will either be names of a person, a location, expressions of times, organizations, quantities, monetary values, or percentages that will be counted as a term. This would include any of their known iterations when looking through the documents. An example of this would be:

G.O.T. or GOT for *Game of Thrones.*

NY Mets for New York Mets.

These are just a few examples with the abbreviations, and the named entity extraction would ensure finding the right words, even if the user went with a different way to write it out.

This approach is very intensive of the knowledge that it provides. Moreover, it will work well if the person has been trained on a large number of documents or if you hand code it to have the knowledge that you want with all of these different names.

Data mining text can provide a unique challenge when working on mining information that you want. However, since the text can provide a lot of important information to the business about their customers and the products and services that they provide, it is still really valuable to have. You can choose to use one of the methods above to ensure that you get the right information that you need, based on what you are looking for, to make some great business decisions.

Chapter 6: Basic Machine Learning Algorithms to Know

Algorithms are going to play a big role in all the stages when working on data science. It is used to mine valuable data from any type of data, including the unstructured form of text. It is further even used to organize structured data. And, more importantly, it is there to create and then test models that the business would use to create the solutions needed for various situations.

With the help of machine learning, all of this is done automatically. This is why you should learn some of the algorithms for machine learning if you would like to be able to work with data science.

Going through all of the information on your own is not always going to be the most efficient use of your time. If there is a large amount of data to sort through, it can take up too much time. Or you may end up missing out on things because there is just too much information to go through.

This is where algorithms come in. They are going to do a lot of the work for you to ensure you find the exact kind of information that you need, no matter what it is and no matter how much data you want to go through.

What are algorithms?

These are complex codes that give instructions. They can do this for helping to complete a task or solve a problem and can be set up to be completely automated or at least partially automated. It is an independent sequence of actions that have been designed to accomplish the purpose needed and, in this case, it is problem-solving. It also has the capability of performing calculations, data processing, and doing automated reasoning tasks.

Basically, the algorithms that we are going to take a look at are there to help give the system the directions that you need to start. You can memorize these algorithms or put them somewhere safe so you can pull them up when you need to use them.

Linear regression algorithm

This is originally from statistics and is one of the best known and most used algorithms when using machine learning. It will model the relationship between the scalar dependent variable that is denoted as y and one or more independent variable that is denoted as x. When we are working with machine learning, this is the one that is used to make sure that the predictive ability of a model is improved because it uses historical data. For the most part, the linear regression will be a supervised algorithm.

k-Nearest Neighbors

This one can also be denoted with the k-NN. This algorithm stores all the cases needed and classifies the new cases by going with the similarity measure. It will be used to help with both regression and classification predictive problems. A common application used with this would be, *Will a customer pick this product? Would it be good to target them for a certain type of advertising? And is it possible to develop more business with that customer?* All of these are important things to understand how to work with when running a business, and the k-NN algorithm can help out with this.

k-means

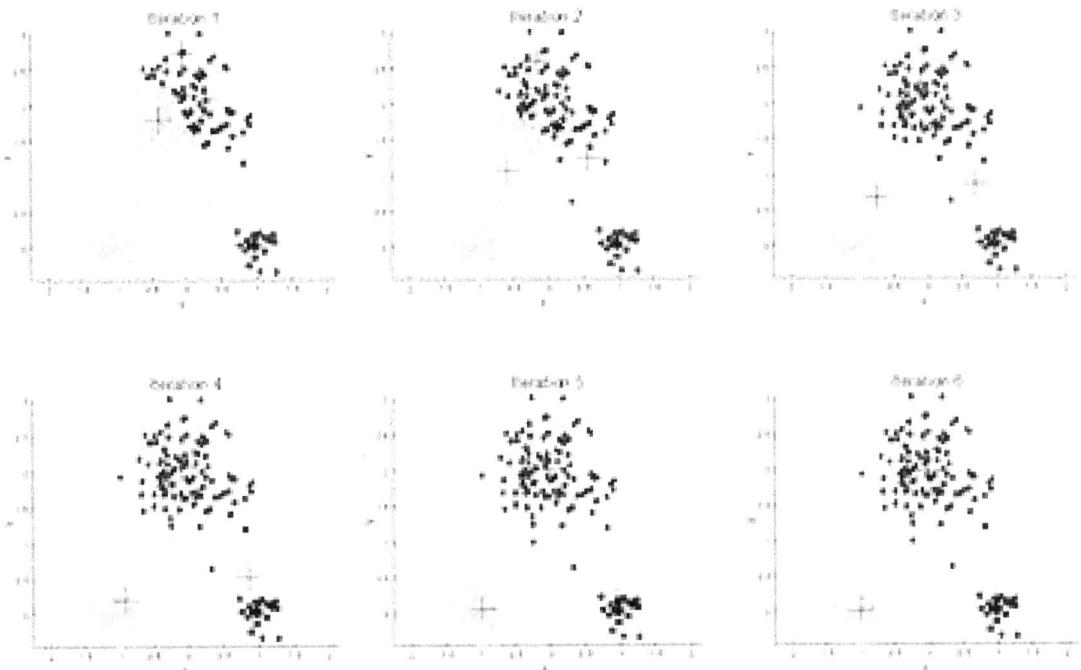

This is another algorithm that is part of unsupervised learning. It is responsible for finding groups inside of data. The *k* stands for the number of clusters or groups in the data. The algorithm groups data points based on the features that they share in common. This would net results of either grouping of data points that you can label new data, or as training data.

When doing this in business, this kind of algorithm is used to find groups within employees or customers that have not been given a label. This can sometimes work to a business' advantage because, depending on who is in it, it could present a brand-new demographic that can be used to maximize sales. Sometimes, this new demographic may not have even been considered as an option, and other times it may have been researched to see if a customer base fell into it.

If k-means is used to help with categorizing employees, it could end up providing a demographic group that has specific professional or educational backgrounds, and this could end up being the way a business figures out who is the best candidate for a new team inside of the organization. They would be able to go through their personal team already and figure out who is the best fit for that new team, rather than trying to hire someone new or picking the wrong people because they were not able to sort through the information in the right way.

Using algorithms is one of the best ways to work with the large data sets inside of an organization. A business wants to make sure that they can find the specific things that are needed by the organization to get the best results. Using these specific algorithms can make it easier to find exactly what is needed, no matter how large the data set is.

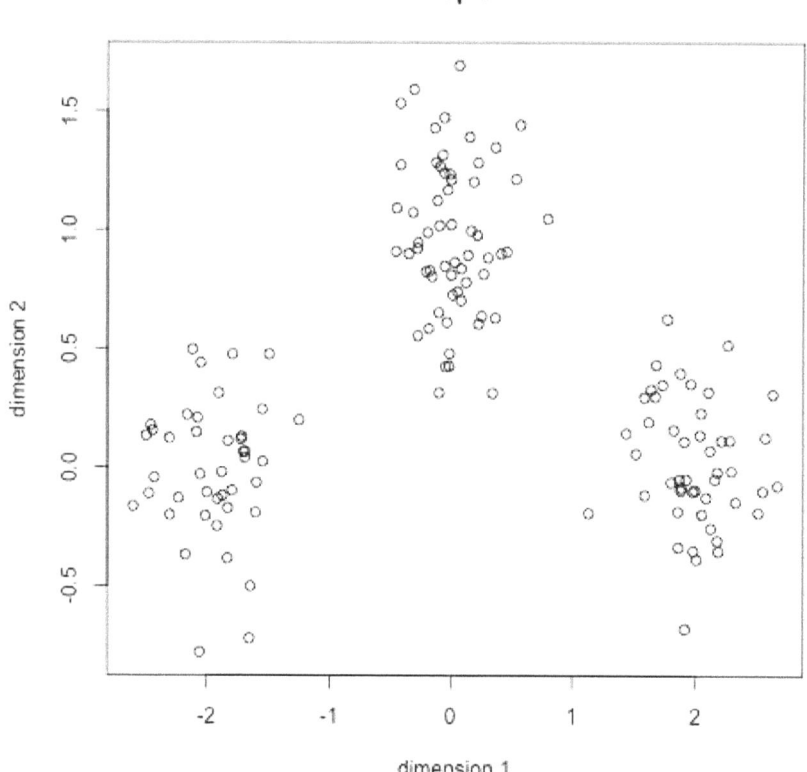

Now we need to look at an example of how this is done:
- To begin, we first select the number of groups or classes that we want to use. Make sure that you initialize their center points randomly for these groups.

- To help you figure out the number of classes that you want to use, you can take a look at the data that you have and see if distinct groups encompass the majority of the data that you have. The center points are vectors of the same length as each data point vector and are your *X's* in the graphic above.
- Each of the data points will be classified simply by computing the distance between that point and the center of each group. You would then classify the point to be in the group where it is closest to one of the centers.
- Based on these points that you chose, you can recompute the group center by taking the mean of all the vectors in your group.
- You would then keep repeating these steps for the set amount of iterations that you want. Or you would keep going until the group centers didn't change much between the iterations.
- Sometimes it is best to randomly initialize the centers a few times and then pick out the run that looks like it provided the best results.

You will find that the k-means have the advantage over some of the other options because it is pretty fast. The only thing that you are doing with it is computing the distance between the points and their group centers. It does not have very many computations to work with, so that makes it a bit easier to get the results that you want.

Mean Shift Clustering

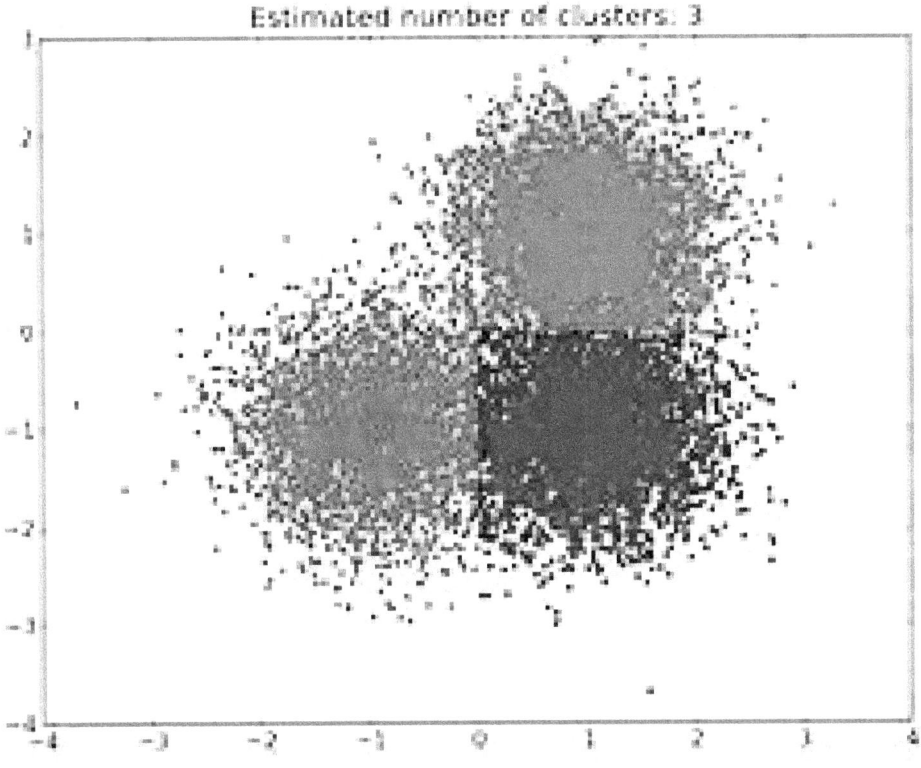

Another option that you can go with is known as mean shift clustering. This is a sliding window-based algorithm that works to find dense areas inside of all your data points. It is also a centroid based algorithm, which just means that the goal of it is to figure out the center points of each class or group and it will work because it can update candidates for the center point to be the mean of the points in your sliding windows.

These particular candidate windows are then filtered during your post-processing stage, so you make sure that you get rid of any duplicates. When you are done, you are going to end up with a final set of center points along with their corresponding groups.

Some of the things that you will need to do to work with the mean shift clustering include:

- To help explain the mean shift, you will need to consider a set of points that are placed in a two-dimensional space. You would begin with a sliding window of a circle that is centered at point C. The point C is one that is randomly chosen, and it will have a radius r as a kernel. Mean shift is a hill climbing algorithm which will involve having you shift the kernel iteratively to a higher density region in each step until you reach convergence.
- At every iteration, this sliding window will shift towards a region that has a higher density. It can this by shifting the center point to the mean of the points that are inside that window.
- The density that is within this sliding window will be proportional to how many points are inside of it. When you do this, you will naturally move towards areas that have more points there.
- You can continue to shift the sliding window by the mean until there isn't a direction or it isn't able to hold onto any more points in your kernel.
- You will repeat the steps above with a lot of sliding windows until you can get all the points inside this window. When you have several windows that overlap, the one that has the most points inside will be the one that is kept.

Density-based spatial clustering of applications with noise (DBSCAN)

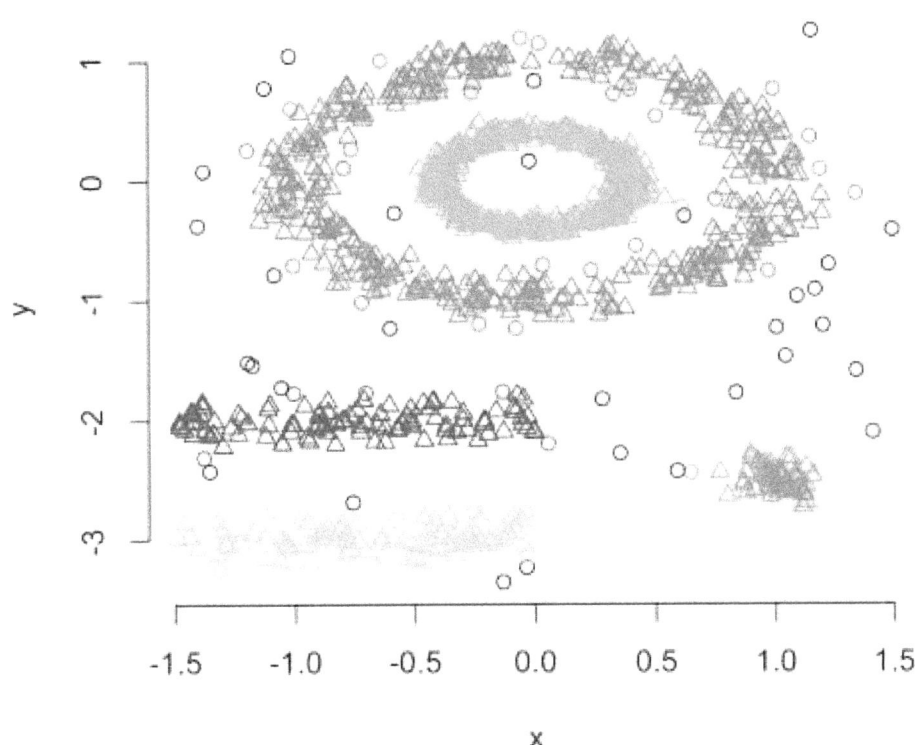

The next type of algorithm that you can work with is known as DBSCAN. This is a clustered algorithm that is based on density. It is similar to what you find with the mean shift, but some advantages come with it. Some of the things that you need to know when working with the DBSCAN include:

- DBSCAN will begin with a starting point that is arbitrary, but which has not been visited. The neighborhood of this point will be extracted using a distance epsilon. This means that all of the points within the epsilon distance will be considered neighborhood points.
- If there are enough points in this neighborhood, then the clustering process will start, and the current data point is known as the first point in your brand-new cluster.
- If there are not enough points, that starting point is labeled as noise. Sometimes it can become a part of another cluster. However, either way, that point will be marked as *visited*.
- For the first point in your new cluster, the points that are within the epsilon distance neighborhood are also going to become a part of that cluster. This procedure will be repeated for all of the new points that were added to the cluster group.

- This process will be repeated until the points are all determined in the cluster. This ensures that all of the points have been visited and labeled as well.
- When you are done with the current cluster, the system will go through and find an unvisited point to start processing. This will keep on happening until all the points are marked, and any that are unattached to a cluster are called noise.

DBSCAN can give you many advantages over some of the other clustering algorithms. First, you do not need to have a specific number of clusters to make it happen. It can also identify the outliers as noise, so they don't just get thrown in and mess up some of the results.

The biggest negative that comes with using DBSCAN is that it won't perform as well as some of the other algorithms when the clusters come in at varying density. This is because the setting of the distance threshold can make it difficult. This drawback will occur data is high-dimensional.

Expectation-Maximization (EM) Clustering with the help of Gaussian Mixture Models (GMM)

One of the major issues that you are going to run into when using k-means is that it is naïve when it uses mean value for the center of your cluster. This isn't always the best way to do things and can make some mixed results. However, you will find that the Gaussian Mixture Models (GMMs) can give you some more flexibility. With GMMs, we can assume that the data points are Gaussian distributed. This helps because it is less restrictive.

To help you find the parameters of the Gaussian for each cluster, or the mean and standard deviation, you will need to use an algorithm that is known as the Expectation Maximization or EM. To do this, you will need to follow these steps:

- To begin, you will need to select how many clusters you would like and then randomly initialize the distribution parameters of Gaussian for the clusters. You can try to come up with a good estimate of this to help set up the initial parameters just by looking at your data if there isn't too much of it.
- Given the Gaussian distributions that you pick for each cluster, you would then want to compute the probability that each data point belongs to a particular cluster. When a point is close to the center, the more likely it is to be in that cluster. This makes a lot of sense if you assume that most of the data you are looking for will lie closest to the center of your cluster.
- Based on this probability, you can compute a new set of parameters so that you are getting the maximum probabilities of data points in those clusters.
- You can compute these new parameters with the help of a weighted sum of the positions of the data points. Here you are going to look at where the weights are and the probabilities of the data point belonging to that cluster.
- This would keep on repeating until you get a convergence where the distributions are going to change much more, if at all, from one iteration to another one.

Two main advantages come from using the GMMs. First, these are more flexible when it comes to the covariance of the cluster. This is because of the standard deviation parameter that allows the clusters to take on any type of ellipses shape rather than having to be in a circle.

Agglomerative Hierarchical Clustering

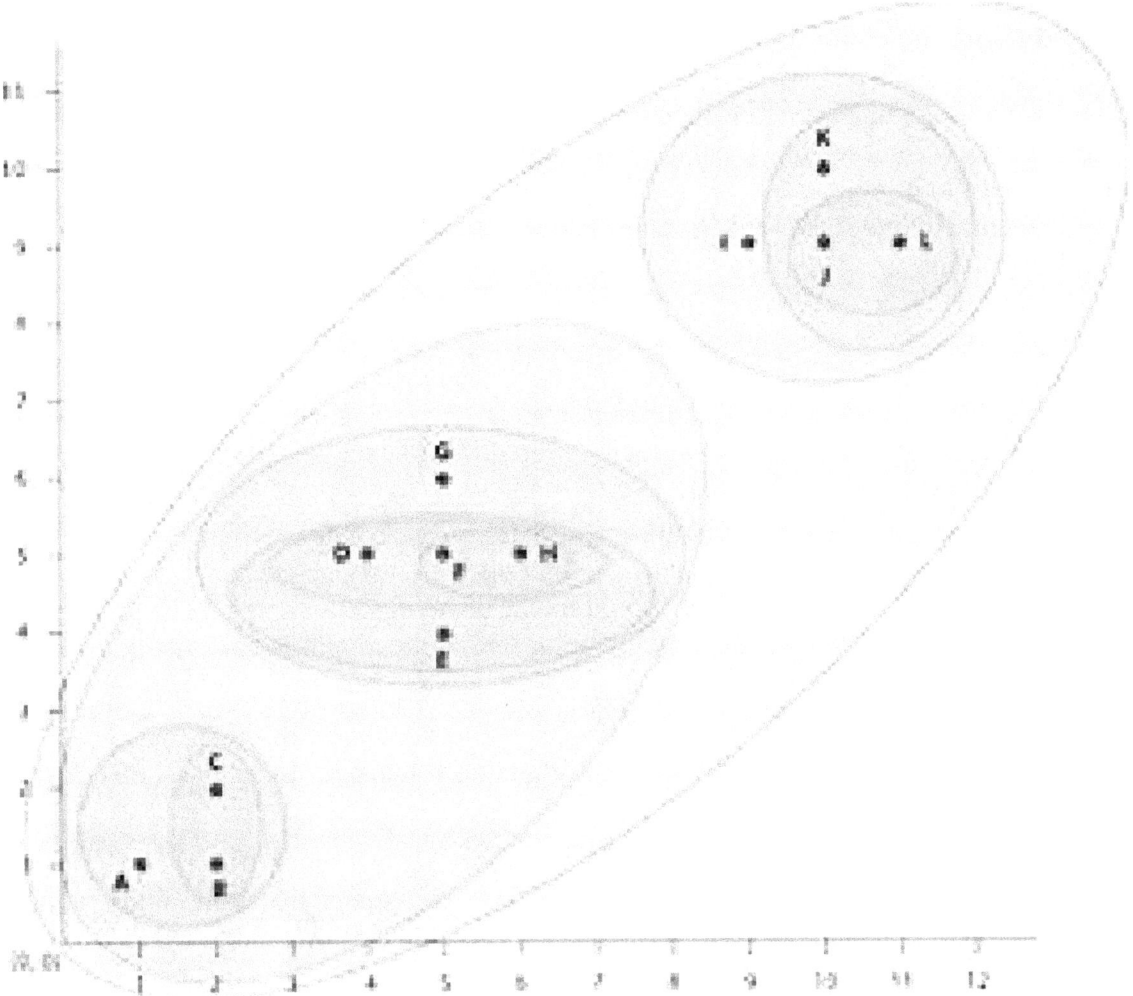

When it comes to using algorithms that are hierarchical, they fall into two categories: bottom-up and top-down.

The bottom-up algorithms are the ones that treat each data point as a single cluster but then will start merging pairs of these clusters. It will continue to do this until you end up with one cluster that will hold onto all of the data points.

The hierarchy of clusters will look like a tree. The root of this tree will be the unique cluster that can gather all of the samples until you end up with just one sample.

There are several steps needed for this clustering:

- You are going to start out by taking each data point and treating it like it belongs to its own cluster. So, if you have 1,000 data points in the data set, then you would start out with 1,000 clusters.
- From here, you are going to select a distance metric. This is there to help measure the distance between two clusters. You will use average linkage which will define the

distance between two clusters to be the distance average between data points that are in the first cluster against those that are in the second cluster.

- With each iteration that you go through, you will end up combining two clusters into one. The two clusters that end up combining will be selected because they are the ones that have the average linkage that is the smallest. This means that they do not have a very large distance between each other and are very similar. This tells the program that they are similar and need to be combined.
- You will continue repeating the steps above until you reach what is known as the root of the tree. This gives you a result where you have one single cluster that will contain all of the data points. So, with the example above, you will start with 1,000 clusters and then end up with just one when this is all done.
- You can use this to pick out how many clusters you would like to end up with. You would tell the program when you would like it to stop – by saying when it should stop combining the clusters. Thus, instead of letting it go down to one, you would decide on five clusters or whatever number you would like.

Hierarchical clustering does not make it a requirement that you pick out how many clusters you would like to use. You can let it keep going until you end up with just one cluster. However, you can go through and add in more clusters if you would like. This works out great if you are looking to separate out the demographics of who shop with you or if you already know how many of these groups you are going to need from the beginning.

In addition, this kind of algorithm is not going to be sensitive to the choice of the distance metric. They are all going to work equally well, while with the other clustering algorithms, the choice of the distance metric will be pretty important.

You will find that working with a hierarchical algorithm is often a good one to use when you have data that is hierarchical in structure, and you want to be able to recover that same thing. Other algorithms for clustering are not able to do this as well as this method. However, you should know that while there are many advantages to using hierarchical clustering, it is not as efficient as some of the other methods. It takes up more time compared to the other methods – so if you are short on time, this may not be the best one for you.

These are just a few of the different types of algorithms that you can use when it comes to working with data science. You will need to have a good idea of the information that you have, as well as what information you want to learn from the data, to help you figure out what algorithm you should go with.

Chapter 7: Data Modeling

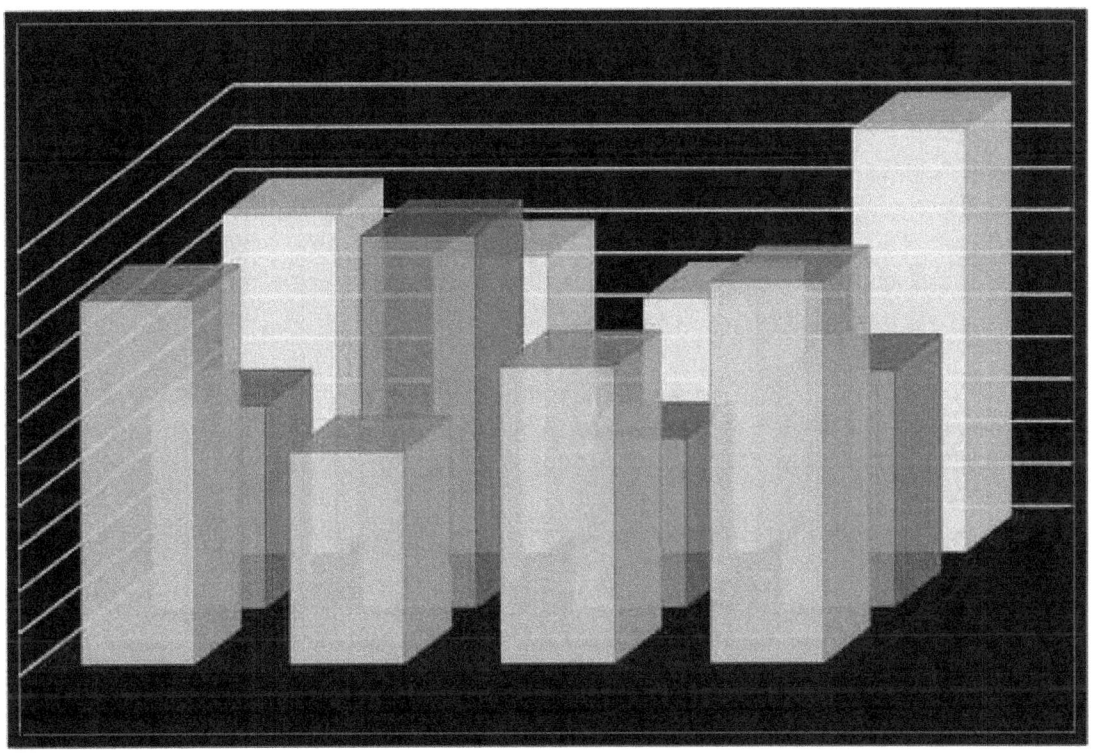

The next topic is known as data modeling. The data science process is always going to provide you with some kind of model. This model is used to report to the management so that they can use it to make some new business decisions. Or it can be used to predict phenomena that could help save the company some money or maximize the opportunities they have with as little risk as possible. Data modeling can do all of this for a company, and we are going to take a closer look at what it is and how you can test the models.

What is a model

A model is a simplified representation of reality created to serve some purpose for the user and which will be based on certain data. The purpose can be several things but is usually there to preserve information that is relevant or to simplify the information even more.

Other than the two things mentioned above, a model can also be used to forecast or predict what will happen in the future, based on the data the company has now, so that the company can make decisions ahead of time to help them increase profits, help customers, provide better products, or at least reduce their risks.

When we are working on data science, these models are there to create a nice picture of the data. It makes the data easier to read so that it is easier to make good decisions from that data. The model is there to provide any explanations that are needed so that the managers can stay on track and avoid big issues. If it is used properly, it will help the business to avoid painful losses that they may have to deal with if they only relied on intuition to make their decisions.

Examples of models

There are a few different types of models that a data scientist can work with to get the results that they want. Some of the options include:

Descriptive model

These show some of the real-world events that are going on as well as the relationships between the factors that can cause these events. This model will be used by a business to help them target the right people when they are marketing and advertising. It will be generated by using statistics to help pick out the differences and the similarities between customer groups. It could help provide many insights based on the purchasing behavior, interests, and demographics (among other things) of the target group.

Linear model

This has a few different options based on the context and how the business would like to use it. It can sometimes be used for time series and regression models. A linear regression model, for example, is there to show the relationship between at least one independent variable and a scalar dependent variable.

Predictive model

This is a formula that is meant to estimate the unknown value of interest. This will come either in a logical statement or a mathematical formula and sometimes it is a combination of the two. These types of models will be created and then tested based on some historical data. A good example is a credit scoring estimate which would use your credit history to predict how likely it is that you would default on a future loan. Or an email service that filters out spam by receiving information from other users on what was reported as spam.

Probabilistic model

This incorporates random variables and probability distributions. The variable that you use here will represent any potential outcomes that can happen for an uncertain event. This will incorporate uncertainty right in the model and can help the business to look over things that are uncertain for them.

Classification model

This designates items in a collection to certain categories or classes that you can specify. It will aim to forecast the target class for items in the data with various properties of an item that is present in the data set. An example is to classify a loan applicant as either low, medium, or high credit risk. Alternatively, with your business, it could be used to classify a customer as an infrequent, frequent, or loyal customer for your company.

Model evaluation techniques

Now that we have looked at some of the most common models that you can use with data science, you will want to learn how to test them. You will test the models before you deploy them into the system or report them back to the management team. This will ensure that it will be applicable even outside of the data set which it was built upon. Some of the different model evaluation techniques that you can use for this include:

- *Confidence interval*: This tests how reliable the statistical estimate is. When the test resulted in a wide confidence interval, this means that the model you are testing will be a poor one or that the data that was used was pretty noisy and messed with the data.
- *Confusion matrix*: This tests the validity of your clustering algorithms. The higher the concentration of observations found in the diagonal of the confusion matrix, the more accuracy there is in that clustering algorithm.
- *Gain and lift chart*: This measures how effective a predictive model is. The effectiveness will be calculated as a ratio between the results that were obtained with the model and the results that were obtained without the model.
- *Kolmogorov-Smirnov chart*: This compares how close two different distributions are to one another. Out of these two distributions, one of them will be a theoretical model of these observations. The other one will be the non-parametric distribution that was computed from your observations.
- *Chi-square*: This is similar to the test above, but is considered a parametric test.
- *ROC curve*: This is a shorter version of what is known as the *receiver operating characteristic curve*. It is a plot on a graph that will test how probable it is that a false alarm will occur with your probability detection.
- *Gini coefficient*: This measures statistical dispersion. It was originally intended to be used to see the inequality of the wealth distribution of a nation's residents.
- *Cross-validation*: This method assesses the performance of the model in the future. It can sometimes be used with model selection.
- *Predictive power*: This is a synthetic metric that is used to choose which subset of features in a specific set of data.
- *Root mean square error*: This is often used because it is good at telling you if there is a goodness of fit. It can be used to test whether your model fits the indicators of reality as recorded by your data.

The data modeling is a good way to take the data and put it in a graph or another form that makes it easier to read through and understand. Being able to do this properly and test it can make a big difference in how well your information can be used. If the modeling is done correctly, you can easily use the data as a way to make predictions and new decisions for your business in the future.

Chapter 8: Data Visualization

Data visualization is important. Even if the data is in a model or a structured format, the data in its basic form can sometimes be hard to make sense of or even turn into a visual representation. Even when it is complicated, the data scientist will at some point need to present their findings over to the management. The management will not need to have the same expertise about the process like a data scientist does, but they do need to be able to understand the information that they are presented with.

It is up to the data scientist to go through and make sure that not only can organize the information that they have from the data, but they can present it in a way that the managers can look over and understand. If the information does not make sense or is hard to read, the managers are going to have a hard time using that information to make good business decisions.

If you are going to make a visual for your boss or manager of a company based on the data that you find, you must make sure that they can read through it properly. If you don't make a good visual, then all the work that you did is worthless. This chapter will take a look at data visualization and what you need to do to get started and make great visuals of the data you find.

Perception and cognition

Variations in orientation, color, length, and shape are things that the human mind can distinguish between. Even if you have a table that shows the trends in domestic and international sales of your product every month, you would want to consider using color or different shapes to show this information. The managers could look closely at it and probably figure it all out, but you want to make sure that it is as easy as possible for them to read through so you would make these changes.

One way to do this is to have the international sales in red and the domestic sales in blue. This helps the observer to see what is going on with the trends of each in just a few seconds. They would then be able to look on your graph to see when the high and low months are for the sales, whether one is falling behind the other, and if any concerns are coming up.

As a data scientist, it is not enough to just go through and look at the information and understand it yourself. You want to make sure that the view to the manager is easy to understand. This will not only make them appreciate your work a bit more but can ensure that they read through the information properly.

To make sure that you take full advantage of the understanding through the perception of the brain, the data that you present should indicate the nature of the relationship between the different variables. It needs to show the quantities that you want accurately through different types of graphs just by looking at them. Moreover, it should also be designed in a way that an observer can easily compare the different quantities through things like colors or labeling.

You need to use the best visual aid possible based on the data that you have. This will vary based on the information that you were looking through for the manager. And it should make it obvious how people should use any of the information that is on your visual aid. Overall, you want to make sure that any visualization of the data is easily judged based on its accuracy, efficiency, ease, and how the story of the information is delivered.

Gestalt Principles of Perception

In business, decisions need to be made as quickly as possible. The decision-makers do not want to spend a ton of time looking through the graph and hoping that they will be able to figure out the information. The reason that they hired a data scientist in the first place is so that they can get through information quickly and easily rather than sifting through it on their own.

A good thing to follow, when you are trying to make graphs and other visuals that are easy to look through, is the *Gestalt Principles of Perception*. This was a result of a study that was done in 1912. It was done to figure out how people perceive organization, form, and pattern. Even today, the results of the study are still accurate.

You will be able to use the basic principles from this idea to make it easier to visualize data from data science. The principles that you need to follow include:

- *Proximity*: Items that you put close together will be seen as one group. If you do not want them to be from the same group, then they need to be spaced apart.
- *Similarity*: Items that are the same shape or color will be seen as one group.
- *Enclosure*: Items that are inside of an illustration and bordered by a line or shape will be one group.
- *Closure*: Any open images or shapes can be seen as complete or regular, and that is how many people will see them.
- *Continuity*: Shapes or items that are brought into line with one another will be seen as one group.
- *Connection*: Items that are interconnected are seen as one group. Be careful how you arrange them to make sure you are grouping the right things.

All of these can be important when you are learning how to group information inside of the graphs that you create. You want to make sure that things that are alike are grouped together, but you also have to make sure that you aren't accidentally grouping things that shouldn't be. When you are creating your graph, take a look at the six principles of perception above and see if you can use them to make your graph more visually appealing to the observer.

How to use diagrams for visualization

There are several different types of diagrams that you can use to showcase the information that you are presenting. The one that you use will depend on the information that you are showing and what will make it look the best. Some of the options that you have when it comes to diagrams include:

- *Line graph*: This visualizes the value of your variable over a period of time. This could be over a few days, months, or even years. The *x-axis* of this graph will represent how much time is covered in the graph, and the *y-axis* is responsible for showing off the amount or the value that you need.
- *Bar chart*: This is responsible for comparing values of different dependent variables in the same independent variable. Your dependent variables can be a variety of things, including the income of your company, production, performance, or how your salespeople or others in the business are doing. You can compare them to each other in the same company or even compare to industry averages.
- *Scatter plot*: This is responsible for visualizing the relationship between the variable (*x-axis*) and another variable (*y-axis*) within multiple periods of time. You can also work with a three-dimensional scatter plot to help showcase the information that you have. This one is created when you just add in a new variable on your *z-axis*. This can be very helpful when working in data science because it allows you to have more variables present.
- *Pie chart*: This visualizes the distribution of groups in a population. You could pull information to find out the age of your customers, and the pie chart would tell you what percentage of your customers fall into each age group. This could be done with many demographics for your customers – what products they like, and more – and will provide some valuable information.
- *Histogram*: This assesses the probability of distribution of a variable. This graph can do this by illustrating the frequencies of observation that will occur within a certain range of values.

All of these graphs can be useful when it comes to putting together the information that you need to present after going through all of the data. Often the type of data that you find will determine which of these graphs is the best one for you. Make sure that whatever one you choose is easy to use, makes sense for the data, and will be easy to put together and look nice in your presentation.

Chapter 9: How to Use Data Science Right

While there is a lot that you can do with data science, you must remember that it is mainly just a tool that you use in business. If you know how to use it properly and you make sure to stay efficient with it, data science can be a great tool that helps limit your risk and even make you more money. However, if you do not use it properly, it could easily cause a lot more harm to your business than it does good.

It is easy to become captivated with all of the possibilities that can come with data science. But if your business can't afford it or if you just try to use it without the right experience or knowledge, then you will end up costing your business a lot of money. The best way to avoid this is to make sure that the data science team and the management team become are aware of some crucial points along the way.

What management needs to know

To get as much out of the wealth of data that a business has, and information on the Internet, management must think of the data analytically. If management is not able to do this, then they will become completely dependent on the results from data mining, and they won't think for themselves. There is a ton of information that comes from the data mining process, but you must think it through and combine your knowledge and expertise to get the best results.

Of course, this is not to say that the management needs to be data scientists to understand the information and to use it. It just means that the managers of an organization at least need to know some of the basics to appreciate the different opportunities that it will provide. You do not want to waste the valuable resources that data science can provide simply because you don't understand how it works or what all it can do for you and your company.

As a manager, there are a few things that you should be able to do, even if you are not a data scientist. You should be able to appreciate all the opportunities that this information provides, make sure that your data science team has the resources that it needs to get the job done and be willing to invest your time and money so that data experimentation occurs. Finally, you must be able to work with your team to ensure that they stay on track and help you get information to help move the business forward.

How data science gives a competitive advantage

Data science, as long as it is used correctly, can give a business a big competitive edge in their market. To have an advantage over the competition, you must make sure that you are always one to two steps ahead of them. This can be done through a willingness and the act of investing in new data assets and also the development of new capabilities and techniques. It also requires that you not only treat the investment and the results from this as an asset, but you must also treat your data science team and the field of data science in the same way.

With the best data science team, you will be able to gain the useful insights that you need to help move your business into the future. There are so many businesses that will just rely on experience and knowledge to help them. And if you have been in the industry for a long time, you will probably do well. Most of those who are new to an industry will end up failing with this though.

However, even if you are doing well, data science could provide you with some useful information and open up new doors that you may not have thought about in the past.

Chapter 10: Tips for Data Science

Getting started in data science is a great idea when you want to make improvements in your business, but you want to make sure that you are making decisions that will be smart – rather than just taking leaps and not knowing what you are doing. Having some tips to make it easier, can make a big difference in the results that you see.

Let's take a look at some of the best tips that you can use when you get started with data science.

Understand the business before starting to solve any problems

While the data scientist may be excited to get started, you have to understand what you are looking for before you can do the work. Otherwise, you may use the wrong method or algorithm, or you are going to just end up with a lot of information that looks like a mess. It is best to understand the business before you take up the project. If you already work for that company and you do this in-house, then it shouldn't be an issue.

Some of the things that you should explore about the business to help you out include:
1. *Customer level information*: You need to have some ideas about the customers the company has. This could be a month on month customer attrition, a number of active customers, and more.
2. *Business strategies*: This would be a look at the way that the company gets new customers and how they work to keep their valuable customers.
3. *Product information*: You also need to have some information on the product or services that the company offers. You can ask how the customer will interact with the products and how they earn money through the product. Learn as much about the product as possible before starting.

If you can go through and answer these questions, then you have a good start to working on the project.

Figure out the right evaluation method you should use

This is not meant to be a difficult puzzle to solve for you as an analyst, but this is also a trap that some will find themselves in.

Let's say that you are doing the data science to come up with a targeting model for a new marketing campaign. You need to know which model you are going to use to get the right information out of your data set.

The best way to figure this out is to take a look at the information that you have and figure out which method would be the best for you. Some types of data are going to lend themselves better to one method over another, and you will see this pretty quickly. Other times, you may have to try a few of the methods to see which one gives you the best results, or at least the results that look the least confusing.

Break out of the industry silos to get alternate solutions

Analytics is being used in almost all business industries. So instead of staying in traditional approaches, that are found with your particular business, why not go beyond that and see if other industries have found the solution that you are looking for.

A good example of this is a recommended video solution that was implemented in the e-commerce industry and can be used when you are doing a blogging portal. However, the only way that you are going to get this done is to interact with those who are working in the other industry. This can help you to learn how to make it happen and learn from them.

If you just sit there in your own industry and try to get things done, you may see some success, but you are missing out on some great opportunities. Our world is changing quickly, and many industries are using the same technology in different ways. Learning how some of these industries use data science can end up helping your own business, even if they are not really related.

Engage with your business counterparts

You should not be doing the whole analysis on your own. This will make you miss out on many important things. You must interact with other business partners and discuss what they are looking for, some of the important things about their business, and so on. As you go through the process, you should make sure that you keep in touch with them.

Sometimes this is hard. When you do the analysis for a business, they often want to stay away from the technical details because they are worried that these details would be too complicated. They would be just happy to receive the results at the end and then go through them and make decisions. However, if you want to do the best analysis possible, you must have a constant stream of interaction between you and the people you do the work for. This helps you to stay on track through it, find the right information, and even find some patterns that you may miss out on if you do the whole project on your own.

Keep the language simple

You do not need to dumb down the information so that it is watered out, but some statisticians like to use complex formulations that those people outside of the field cannot understand. Moreover, this is even easier to do when you work with data science. However, what you need to do is look at the output of variables that you have and then try to find a simple way to help the business understand what you are presenting to them.

Let's take a look at how this can work:

You are looking through the data that you have to find out which agents would be the top performers once they got onboard the team. You may come up with the right stratified population and the way that you expect them to perform based on the data. In the process, you had to go through and choose a lever which may have changed the population mix. What you would do here is simple. You would just need to implement a differential fee strategy so that you could change the application mix and then this would change the population mix.

During this process, you would also want to make sure that you learn the business language when you are presenting your findings to business leaders. The project may be easy, but sometimes you may have trouble selling it back to a business. And often the reason for this is because of the gap in understanding the internal discussions with the business.

It is really important for you to speak the language of your audience. It is possible to have times when the smartest models are rejected, and the simple models are the ones that the company likes. The only reason for this is because the analyst can speak business to the company while presenting their models.

Follow up on the chosen implementation plan

So, after you have gone through and talked to a business about the model you want to use for this process, there is still more work to be done. You need to set up some monthly (or more often if needed) follow-ups with the business to help understand how the project was implemented and that it is being used in the right manner.

You want to make sure that the business is on board with what you are doing and that they are being presented with the most up-to-date information possible. They will not want to receive the information just once and then call that good forever. The world of business is changing so fast that information they find valuable today may not count in a few weeks or months. A constant flow of new data will come in, and setting up meetings with the business and those in charge on a regular basis will make it easier to ensure that they get the best and newest information to make important business decisions.

Read about the industry

The industry is always changing and growing. While something may have been difficult to do in the past, in a few months, it may be really easy because a new technique has developed. You can learn from others in the field and even rely on some of the other industries which use this science to provide you with the solutions that you need.

As you get started with the industry of data science, make sure that you read as much as possible to help you out. You can look at books, look online, look at magazines, and more. The more information that you can learn about the industry, the better you can be at providing data science services to your clients. Never stop learning. This industry will change a lot in the near future and having a lot of knowledge readily available, and ensuring that you keep up-to-date, can be really valuable when you are first getting started. You never know what you can learn along the way that could help make your job a whole lot easier.

Find new ways to improve

The field of data science is growing by leaps and bounds. It is a relatively new field, but it is really helping many businesses to grow and do well. The only issue is that since it is so new, it is growing so quickly and you will find that many new techniques and even new methods are going to come out in the future. These can really improve what you can do in data science, but it means that you will always need to update your skills along the way.

If you are working on a project and find that none of your techniques from the past seem to be just right, then you may want to consider doing some research. There are always new ways that you can try out, and it is certain that more will be introduced in the near future. Never stop learning about the industry and what it has to offer and continue to learn more of the techniques along the way. This will ensure that you are providing your clients with the best information possible and it can even make your work so much easier.

Do not make the decisions for the company

Unless you are one of the managers in the company who has started doing data science, you do not get to make decisions for the company, and you do not get to push what ideas you think would be the best. Your job is to provide information for the company efficiently and quickly. You will, of course, write a report on the information that you find, and in a way that those in charge of decision-making can read through and see what the best course of action is. But you must only write down what is actually there, without any swaying or changing of the information and without giving your opinion.

The company that hires you is not there to hear your opinion about the market or about what they should do next. They can get opinions all over the place if they want. They want you to go through a large amount of data and information to help them figure out what steps they should take to better their business in the future. If you can do this with a data set and present it in a clear manner, you will do well with the business.

Getting started in data science can be a rewarding and exciting career choice. Many companies are starting to see the value of hiring individuals, or at least training ones in their own company, who can go through all this information to help them make informed decisions.

Moreover, when these companies find someone who can give them accurate information, they can combine it with their own experience and knowledge about the industry to help move their company into the future.

Conclusion

I hope this book has provided you with all the tools you need to achieve your goals.

The next step is to get started using the new skills that you learned about data science. Data science is a newer field of study that many businesses are quickly learning is important in helping them out. When it is combined with knowledge and experience in a specific industry, it can be one of the best ways to ensure that you make great and profitable business decisions. Going through all the data on your own, especially if it is large, can be a challenge sometimes. But data science shows you the different methods that you can use to get this done quickly and efficiently.

This guidebook has gone over the basics of what you need to know to get started with data science. We looked at what data science is, what it can be used for, some of the different techniques that you can use with it, and even how to work with the algorithms and the data modeling of some of your projects.

Now, you should be well on your way to understanding what data science is and how you can use it in your own business to make great business decisions.

When you are ready to collect and analyze large amounts of data for your company, and use it to learn more about your business and your customers, make sure to refer to this guidebook.

Finally, if you found this book useful in any way, a review on Amazon is always appreciated!

Thanks for your support!

Check out another book by Herbert Jones